Opposing Censorship in the Public Schools: Religion, Morality, and Literature

Opposing Censorship in the Public Schools: Religion, Morality, and Literature

June Edwards
SUNY Oneonta

LEA LAWRENCE ERLBAUM ASSOCIATES, PUBLISHERS
1998   Mahwah, New Jersey   London

Lawrence Erlbaum Associates, Inc., Publishers
10 Industrial Avenue
Mahwah, New Jersey 07430

Library of Congress Cataloging-in-Publication-Data

Edwards, June, 1934–
Opposing censorship in the public schools : religion,
morality, and literature / June Edwards.
     p. cm.
   Includes bibliographical references and index.
   ISBN 0-8058-2545-2 (alk. paper). — ISBN 0-8058-
2546-0 (pbk.)
    1. Education and state—United States. 2. Public
schools—United States—Curricula—Censorship.
3. Literature—Study and teaching—United States.
4. Teaching—United States—Religious aspects. 5.
Christianity and politics—United States. I. Title.
   LC89.E38 1998
   379.2'8—dc21   97-26311
                                   CIP

[There are] 256 separate and substantial religious bodies . . . in the United States. Each of them . . . has as good a right to demand that the courts compel the schools to sift out of their teaching everything inconsistent with its doctrine. If we are to eliminate everything that is objectionable to any of these warring sects or inconsistent with any of their doctrines we will leave public education in shreds.

—Justice Jackson
McCollum v. Board of Education
333 U.S. 203 (1948)

The mere exposure to ideas contrary to one's religion is not tantamount to compelled belief.

—Mozert v. Hawkins County, TN,
Board of Education
827 F.2d 1058 (6th Cir. 1987)

*This book is dedicated to my children,
Jennifer, Emily, and Jonathan,
and my grandson Jared.
Keep reading!*

Contents

Preface

I first became involved in censorship issues in the mid-1970s while living in southwest Virginia and working on a doctorate, which resulted in my dissertation on value conflicts in public education (Edwards, 1977). Although as a former English and social studies teacher I was aware of attempts to remove books, like many educators I was apathetic about the situation. I assumed that these were isolated incidents mostly in the South, brought about by a few individuals on the fringe, and nothing to worry about in most communities.

My eyes were opened when across the border in Kanawha County, West Virginia, a full-scale book battle erupted in 1974.[1] Striking coal miners vented their economic frustrations on something they could more easily influence: the reading materials given their children, which contained many modern and multicultural selections. In protest over these "immoral" and "filthy" books, schools and businesses were boycotted, angry rallies were held, shots were fired, cars were burned, several schools were vandalized and another one, plus the Board of Education building, were dynamited. The superintendent (who resigned and became a neighbor of mine in Virginia) received threatening phone calls against his family, and right-wing ministers prayed for the death of three protextbook members of the Board of Education.

Invited to give leadership in this affray was a Texas couple named Mel and Norma Gabler, who formed an organization called Educational Research Associates and who have dedicated their lives for more than 35 years to attacking textbooks, public education, and teachers. They have been joined in recent times by a number of other Religious Right (RR) groups, both national and regional, that are well organized, well funded, and exert political power in high places. Far from being random, grassroots incidents by a few individuals in the South, censorship attempts have been made over the years in all states and are often instigated, directed, and given

---

[1]For opposing descriptions of this controversy, see F. Parker, *The battle of the books: Kanawha County (1975)*, Bloomington, IN: Phi Delta Kappa fastback; and J.C. Hefley, *Textbooks on trial (1977)*. Wheaton, IL: Victor Books.

financial support by skillfully run national organizations. Frequently targeting small school districts with strapped budgets, these challenges have wrecked teachers' careers and wreaked havoc with school budgets, as well as disrupted the education of thousands of students.

My interest in the religion side of the censorship debate stems from a 2-year stint as a religious education director in a Methodist church, a year of study at the Chicago Theological Seminary, 2 years working for the national public relations office called Methodist Information, a 34-year marriage to a New Testament professor, attendance at scholarly conferences and presentations on biblical studies, 3 years of teaching in a Jesuit university, and my own participation in Methodist, Lutheran, and now Unitarian Universalist churches.

What I find most disturbing about the attacks on schools and literature by RR extremists is the assertion that they alone know God's will, their literal reading of the Bible is the only correct interpretation, and only those who are *born again* are truly Christian. All others who claim that title, who may be actively involved in various mainstream denominations but do not share the right-wing religious and political agendas, are either terribly misguided or dupes of the devil. And of course those affiliated with a non-Christian faith or with none at all are beyond redemption.

Because only 14% of the U.S. population identify themselves as aligned with the RR, according to an August 1996 Gallup poll (cited in "Some want," 1996), it follows that most public school educators do not ascribe to the RR beliefs and are thus doing the work of Satan and corrupting America's youth through the curriculum, teaching strategies, and most of all, reading materials.

For almost 20 years I have taught graduate courses in history and philosophy of education, school law, and current issues of education. When giving in-service workshops and discussing censorship with students, who are mostly experienced teachers, I have found that despite their belief in the value of what they assign for reading, they are easily intimidated by a charge from a RR proponent that a book is "immoral," "antireligious," or "antifamily." Even though the objection is from one parent, the incident is happening in another school district, or the teacher believes the charge is absurd, the tendency is to stop using the work or to select something more benign but of lesser quality. In addition, librarians may elect to remove a book from the shelves, place it in a restricted area, or decide not to purchase something despite high recommendations by literary critics.[2]

These teachers and librarians are understandably worried about confrontation with a parent or public humiliation. They fear being reprehended, suspended, or even fired by administrators and school boards

---

[2]See Wayne Homstad's *Anatomy of a book controversy* (1995) as an illustration of the effect on teachers and librarians who have experienced a public challenge to an assigned book.

determined not to get entangled in a protracted battle with a few constituents or, worse, in an expensive lawsuit backed by one of the national well-to-do right-wing organizations. The fears are legitimate, but caving in so easily to aggressive critics merely gives censors the incentive to go farther and attack all other books until little of value is left to read. Intimidation and threats are the censors' biggest and most effective weapons.

My purpose in writing this book, therefore, is to encourage educators and school board members to stand up to the charges levied against respected literature by examining the moral elements from the perspective of a more mainstream viewpoint. The RR do not represent the majority of Christians in our country, let alone all the other religions in our society. The examples I give concerning morality in literature, although by no means the only interpretations, serve to demonstrate how the beliefs of many Americans on what is moral and religious and biblical can be considerably different from those of the RR.

The debate over censorship encompasses far more than a conflict over "dirty words" in a particular book. It involves widely differing viewpoints concerning the Constitution, democracy, humanism, Christianity, and the Bible, as well as the purpose of education and literature. To understand the reasons behind the attacks on schools and books and to prepare effective means for counteracting them, we must examine both sides of each of these areas, albeit briefly.

This book is not intended, however, to be a balanced argument. My biases clearly run counter to RR views. The claims are presented, as best I understand them, and largely in the words of the most visible and strident critics, in order to make clear what is being said against teachers and books, and to show the RR's scathing hostility to state-run schools and the determination to tear down public education and replace it with sectarianism.

In the Introduction, vitriolic statements by well-known RR leaders about public schools, teachers, books, programs, and teaching strategies are quoted to illustrate the depth of their dislike for government-sponsored education. Also noted are their openly proclaimed goals for taking over public schools and their plans for achieving this.

Chapter 1 presents the debate about government and religion, including the First Amendment's religion clause and the argument over the separation of church and state. Also noted are several Supreme Court cases regarding religion and public schools to show how the justices have applied the neutrality concept in specific situations.

Chapter 2 discusses the conflict over the meaning of *humanism*, particularly *secular humanism*, which is central to the RR's antischool rhetoric, and also shows the relation between humanism and the principles of democracy that undergird the philosophy of public education.

In chapter 3, the debate about the purpose of reading literature is examined. At issue is whether students should be encouraged to read widely and broaden their knowledge of other cultures, lifestyles, and beliefs, or whether their minds as well as their behavior should be tightly controlled, at least until adulthood.

Because scriptural passages are frequently used as the basis for the charge of immorality and antireligion in challenged books, chapter 4 presents alternative perspectives on the Bible's origin and moral themes. I do not claim to be an authority, although I have had close connections for many years to biblical scholars. The point here is that teachers and students do not need to bow to those who insist on a literal reading and who reject all other interpretations, as well as decades of modern biblical scholarship.

In chapter 5, some of the RR charges frequently made against literature books in general, as well as the reasons given, are presented. Although I disagree with the right-wing views, and at times find them ridiculous, I do believe the critics are sincere in their concerns. They have the freedom to express their opinions, but because they sometimes do great damage to public schools and the education of other people's children, I believe their statements need to be confronted and refuted by views more in keeping with democratic principles. For the most part I state the RR charges in my own words as I understand their reasoning from years of listening to speeches and television debates and reading articles, books, and letters to the editor. But also included are direct quotes where appropriate.

In chapters 6 through 11 some typical charges against six books commonly used in English classes and some counterdefenses are presented. The RR has deemed these books anti-Christian, antireligious, immoral, and unbiblical and fought to have them removed from school classrooms and libraries. The purpose of this section is to counter these views by others that are more progressive, more scholarly, and more in line with the religious beliefs of the majority of Americans, including those who belong to Christian denominations.

Biblical passages are used periodically to demonstrate not only what I see as the primary moral messages in the Bible, but to show that one can find whatever one wants, to prove whatever point one wishes to make. Although the RR will no doubt view this as "the devil quoting Scripture" (while viewing their own selective quotations as a sign of godliness), neither they nor any other group owns the Bible. We are all free to come to our own conclusions about what constitutes biblical morality and how to apply this to our lives and the books we read.

Each book in Part II has been chosen because it highlights a particular issue the critics find objectionable, in addition to the "usual suspects" of language, sexual references, and nonorthodox religious beliefs.

Slaughterhouse-Five by Kurt Vonnegut is an indictment of the bombing of Dresden, Germany, during World War II and contains an antiwar message as well as elements of science fiction and fantasy.

The Catcher in the Rye by J. D. Salinger reflects the problems of male adolescence, hypocrisy, and a family's way of dealing with death and love.

The Grapes of Wrath by John Steinbeck, the story of the *Dust Bowl* migration of destitute families from Oklahoma to California, tackles the issue of oppression, government responsibility, and labor organization.

To Kill a Mockingbird by Harper Lee involves racism and justice in a small Southern town and the courage of a White lawyer to stand up for his moral and religious principles.

Of Mice and Men by John Steinbeck revolves around mental disability and male bonding and raises the issue of mercy killing as a moral act.

I Know Why the Caged Bird Sings by Maya Angelou, a biography of the author's early years, describes her growing up Black and female in a nontraditional family that nurtured her independence, creativity, and resilient strength.

The books are not perfect. None ever are. Nor are all of them suitable for all ages, levels of maturity, and reading ability. Some books that have outstanding qualities that will enhance the lives of students may also contain elements that critics other than the RR find troublesome. Sexism, for instance, is a frequent problem. John Steinbeck's female characters are often superficially drawn, tending toward earth mothers, vamps, or mindless creatures.

Many adult readers find Holden Caulfield in *The Catcher in the Rye* to be an irritatingly immature adolescent, who should stop whining, be more responsible, and appreciate his good fortune. Some teachers and parents might also prefer less vulgar language and explicit sexuality or less use of racial or ethnic slurs in books they otherwise believe are very worthwhile.

Chapter 12 offers suggestions to teachers, administrators, and school board members on how to prevent conflicts over literature books in classrooms and libraries and how to respond professionally to individual objections and public confrontations when they happen anyway.

How a teacher prepares the class and handles the classroom discussions is often critical to a book's acceptance. As noted, students and parents should be given the opportunity to choose an alternate book in lieu of the one assigned to the class if they have objections.

The appendices provide a list of articles and book chapters by other writers on dealing with challenges, a sample complaint form, and a list of addresses of national education and anticensorship organizations.

The books discussed in Part II are filled with the humor, drama, and pathos of human lives and demonstrate that moral issues are an integral part of living in this world. For many people, the choices they make are based on religious convictions, either consciously or intuitively. Readers' reactions to these works will be highly influenced by their own religious outlook.

Most books worth reading will confront readers with moral dilemmas and engage them in issues saturated with religious implications. The

American public school, with its religiously diverse clientele and its commitment to open discussion, is an excellent arena for airing a variety of beliefs, analyzing their impact on human behavior, and aiding students in the discovery of their own convictions.

ACKNOWLEDGMENTS

In writing this book I am grateful to my former husband, Dr. Richard A. Edwards, a New Testament professor at Marquette University, who taught me about biblical scholarship, and Dr. Robert C. Small, Jr., and Dr. Thomas C. Hunt, who first involved me in the topic of censorship when I was a graduate student at Virginia Tech. Both have remained good friends and supportive mentors.

I also appreciate the thoughtful comments and helpful advice given on earlier versions of this book by Dr. Small, now dean of education and human development at Radford University in Virginia, Dr. Daniel C. Maguire, professor of ethics in the Theology Department at Marquette University, Dr. Nicholas J. Karolides, Professor of English at Wisconsin–River Falls, and Dr. Daniel Sheridan, Professor of English, University of North Dakota. I wish to thank also Dr. Anna Stave, my friend and colleague at SUNY-College Oneonta, who critiqued portions of the manuscript and gave much moral support.

A special thanks goes to my editor, Naomi Silverman, for her encouragement and suggestions, and to Lawrence Erlbaum Associates for their willingness to publish a forthright book on sensitive issues related to religion, morality, public schools, and literature.

My ideas have been honed, in addition, by many students and colleagues at the various colleges where I have taught, by teachers and administrators, and by numerous others who have written and spoken about church–state issues, censorship, and the impact of the RR.

Finally, I am grateful to my parents for encouraging reading at an early age and allowing me unlimited access to books, and to the teachers of my own children who introduced them to good literature they might otherwise have missed.

Introduction

For some years, critics of public schools have zealously attacked literature assigned in classrooms and available in school libraries. By labeling books *humanistic* and *antireligious*, they have often been successful in their attempts to ban or limit access to works that many educators feel benefit students intellectually and morally. According to the 1994–1995 report by People for the American Way (1995), there were 458 challenges in 49 states that year to books used in public schools. States with the highest number were California, Texas, and Pennsylvania. Only Hawaii had no reported incidents. The success rate for censorship—that is the removal of or restricted access to books—was nearly 50%.

Underlying the attacks by the RR on literature is a great hostility toward public schools in general and government's involvement in education of any kind. For instance, Pat Robertson (1993), who heads the Christian Coalition, one of the best organized and most powerful political groups in the nation, and owns the Christian Broadcasting Network (CBN), the world's largest television ministry with programs airing in 70 countries, has called schools "crime-infested scandals" (p. 130). He asserted in one of his highly popular "The 700 Club" broadcasts:

> The state steadily is attempting to do something that a few states other than the Nazis and the Soviets have attempted to do, namely, to take the children away from the parents and to educate them in a philosophy that is amoral, anti-Christian, and humanistic and to show them a collectivist philosophy that will ultimately lead toward Marxism, socialism, and a communistic type of ideology. (May 13, 1984, cited in Boston, 1996b, p. 168)

In *The Turning Tide*, Robertson (1993) stated that "in today's education scarcely any facts are being imparted and absolutely no morality" (p. 213).

According to journalist David Mizner (1996), who as part of his job spent many hours watching "The 700 Club," Robertson continually rails on this tax-exempt television program against the evils of public education. In September 1993 he told his viewers that "Satan has established certain strongholds....He has gone after [public] education and has been very successful in capturing it," and "radical lunatics" in these schools are exposing students to corpses, teaching bestiality and witchcraft, and developing curricula "that are destroying the minds of our children" (p. 12).

In a similar vein, television preacher John Hagee called public schools "the most dangerous place you can send your child" (cited in Conn, 1996d, p. 5). Another televangelist, D. James Kennedy, blamed all of our nation's social problems on a "godless educational system" (cited in Conn, 1996d, p. 5).

Tim LaHaye (1982), who established the Coalition for Traditional Values, stated in *The Battle for the Family*, "Modern public school education is the most dangerous single force in a child's life," for those who teach in public schools "have rejected all responsibility for inculcating moral values and character building" (pp. 89, 215). In *The Battle for Public Schools*, LaHaye (1983) claimed that such schools "have become conduits to the minds of youth, training them to be anti-God, antimoral, antifamily, anti-free enterprise, and anti-American" (p. 13).

His wife Beverly LaHaye, head of the influential Concerned Women for America, proclaimed in a speech at a Family Forum Conference that public schools are "taking our children...and filling their minds with information that will destroy Christianity if we let this continue in our country" (cited in *Religious Right gears up*, 1988). In their jointly written book, *Against the Tide* (1993), the LaHayes charged, "Our children are being deceived by secular humanist philosophy and amoral tradition instead of being fortified with Christian principles and moral traditions...in most instances the public school is an unfit place for our children to get their education" (pp. 40–41).

Robert Simonds, founder of the ultra-right Citizens for Excellence in Education, claimed that those promoting a New Age religion have taken over the public schools and want to destroy children's faith in God and "open their minds to seances and witchcraft" (cited in Kaplan, 1994, K7). Michael Farris, the attorney for the school censorship case, *Mozert v. Hawkins County, TN, Board of Education* (1987), in a *New York Times* interview labeled public education a "godless monstrosity" (cited in Kaufman, 1994, p. 49). And Ezola Foster of Black Americans for Family Values declared at a Christian Coalition conference that "our schools have gone from being academic learning centers to socialist training camps" (cited in Bradley, 1995, p. 7).

In their longtime crusade against textbooks, the Gablers of Texas have greatly influenced what publishers put in, or more often leave out of, school books. They asserted that "crime, violence, immorality and illiteracy...the seeds of decadence are being taught universally in schools," and what they are fighting against is "mental child abuse" (cited in Martin, 1982, p. 151). In their book *What Are They Teaching Our Children?* (1985), which is still popular with RR followers, the Gablers claimed that public schools are on a "crusade to censor from texts the Judeo-Christian virtues of family affection, respect of parents, work, thrift, independence, and achievement" (p. 92). Because children are taught that there are no moral absolutes, the result is "rising sexual promiscuity, vandalism, drug abuse, thefts, assaults, drunken driving, and suicides" (p. 99).

Phyllis Schlafly (1984), head of Eagle Forum, laid out in her book, *Child Abuse in the Classroom*, the RR objections to public schools and books in explicit detail:

> Violent and disturbing books and films; materials dealing with parental conflict, death, drugs, mental illness, despair, and anger; literature that is mostly negative and depressing; requiring the child to engage in the role-playing of death, pregnancy, abortion, divorce, hate, anger and suicide; personal attitude surveys and games (such as Magic Circle) which invade the private thoughts of the child and his family; psychological games which force the child to decide who should be killed (such as the Survival Game); explicit and pornographic instruction in sex acts (legal and illegal, moral and immoral); and a deliberate attempt to make the child reject the values of his parents and his religion. (p. 14)

Schlafly targeted psychology and health books, drug and sex education, and programs aimed at promoting self-esteem. She objects to anything that can be viewed as an invasion of privacy or an undermining of parental authority—such as asking students for their opinions, or encouraging them to analyze their own values and behaviors or that of historical figures or characters in books. She opposes journal writing, role-playing, creative writing, and the use of imagination or visualizations.

Schlafly also assailed a highly acclaimed course proposal called "Facing History and Ourselves" that was designed to teach about the Holocaust and the rise of Nazism, calling it "child abuse" and charging that it promoted "psychological manipulation" and "induced behavioral change" (cited in *Facing history*, 1989, p. 1). She claimed that AIDS education in schools amounts to teaching "safe sodomy" (cited in Kropp, 1987), and objects to any matters related to the self, such as self-respect or self-actualization, which she believes places oneself at the center rather than God.

In May 1996, Pat Buchanan, a candidate for the GOP presidential nomination, held a 2-day conference in Washington, DC, called "Winning the Culture War." The goal of his organization, American Cause, is to "take back America," by taking over the arts, the press, higher education, and most of all public schools, which he believes have become disaster zones, destroyed by court decisions and the duplicity of school personnel (cited in *American Cause*, 1996). He asserted at a political rally that God and the Bible have been replaced in public schools with *Playboy* and condoms and said, "We don't need some miserable secular humanist in sandals and beads at the Department of Education telling us how to educate America's children" (cited in Conn, 1995, p. 7).

I want to make a distinction, however, between these right-wing extremists who are bent on eliminating public schools, and others who hold evangelical or fundamentalist religious beliefs but merely have concerns about what their own children are doing or learning in school. These are two separate groups and should not be confused or lumped together.

The second group consists of parents who are very involved with their children and schools. They may object to particular books or assignments, which is certainly their right to do, but are cooperative, reasonable, and willing to accept alternatives. Parents who take a serious interest in their children's education are what we need more of. Many public schools do—and all of them should—welcome the involvement of these parents and work with them in deciding what is best for students. In fact, a number of religiously conservative people, many of them parents, teach in public schools and have no problem with most of the books used in the classrooms or with school programs such as drug and sex education, peer mediation, or cooperative learning.

The first group of far-right extremists, however, are a grave danger to public education. For many years I have read RR publications and listened to the rhetoric. The leaders declare proudly that their aim is to take over the public schools and make them *Christian*, meaning their narrow, sectarian version of Christianity. They truly feel—and openly state—that public schools are the work of the devil and teachers are pawns used by the government to corrupt the minds and morals of youth. They also believe that government has no business establishing schools in the first place or making educational policy. Although paid for by public taxes, in their opinion all schools should be privately run, preferably by fundamentalist Christian teachers and administrators; hence the big push for *school choice* vouchers for parochial institutions.

At the 1996 "Road to Victory" Christian Coalition conference, Roxanne Premont of the North Carolina Education Reform Association, explained the proposed strategy: "The trick is not to go to vouchers directly. Use an intermediate step that will create a large supply of independent schools, called charter schools. Once vouchers are unleashed these schools can easily be converted to private schools" (cited in Conn, 1996a, p. 7).

A former Pentecostal minister, Skip Porteus, who now heads the First Amendment Studies Center in Great Barrington, Massachusetts,[1] said in an interview that he had in his possession a document published by the National Coordinating Committee, which has representatives from 25 right-wing groups, that "outlines their 20-year plan for Christianizing America...it's in five-year increments. One of the goals they have in writing is to eliminate all public schools by the year 2000" (cited in Reich, 1994, p. 14).

---

[1]Skip Porteus has rejected his fundamentalist background and is now dedicated to promoting First Amendment freedoms, especially of religion.

A brochure published by the Citizens for Excellence in Education states blatantly that its major purpose is "reclaiming the public schools in the name of Christ" (cited in Etzioni, 1996, p. 40). Their 65-page booklet, "How to Elect Christians to Public Office" says, "We need strong school board members who know right from wrong. The Bible, being the only true source on right and wrong, should be the guide of board members" (cited in Bednarek, 1986, p. B-3). The plan for taking over the schools is clearly drawn:

> There are 15,700 school districts in America. When we get an active Christian parents' committee in operation in all districts, we can take complete control of all local school boards. This would allow us to determine all local policy; select good textbooks, good curriculum programs; superintendents and principals. Our time has come! (cited in Bednarek, p. B-3)

Tim and Beverly LaHaye have similar goals: "The present school system is so controlled by the federal government and by misled or even corrupt educators that there is little hope of salvaging it...the only remedy is for churches and Christians to build a new church-controlled school system in every city in America" (LaHaye & LaHaye, 1978, p. 34). Calling public education an "anti-Christian movement," Pat Robertson said, "We can change education in America if you put Christian principles in and Christian pedagogy in. In three years, you would totally revolutionize education in America" (cited in *The Faces*, n. d.)

Patrick J. Reilly of Citizens for Educational Freedom exclaimed at a Christian Coalition rally, "Let's break the teachers' unions, and when we get control of the schools we can do what we want with them" (Conn, 1996a, p. 7). Jerry Falwell, a television evangelist, president of Liberty Baptist College in Lynchburg, Virginia, and former head of the now defunct Moral Majority, once stated, "I hope I live to see the day when, as in the early days of our country, we won't have any public schools. The churches will have taken them over again and Christians will be running them. What a happy day that will be!" (cited in Bollier, 1984, p. 18).

All citizens, of course, have the freedom to speak up, and many people in addition to the RR criticize schools for a variety of reasons besides selected literature. Disagreements result over allocation of money, tax increases, class sizes, extracurricular programs, and building needs. Certainly it is everyone's right in a democracy to express opinions and work for positive change, especially when the upbringing of future citizens is involved. These conflicts will never be permanently won by any group, nor should they be, for the nature of a democracy is to be in a continual state of reevaluation and change. Sometimes, however, the attacks on schools and books cross the line of democratic debate and become all-out battles to restrict the rights of other people's children and make schools fit a narrow ideology.

From the beginning of our nation, we have been a multireligious society. Only in New England did one denomination, the Puritans, rule over others, joining church and state into a theocracy. The Founding Fathers resoundingly rejected this union and established in the First Amendment the concept of government neutrality toward both religion and nonreligion. RR leaders, however, maintain that such neutrality was not the intent of the framers of the Constitution. The RR's desire to take over public schools is based on a quite different view of the relationship between church and state, as we see in chapter 1.

State-sponsored schools were originally devised by Jefferson to teach children the tenets of democracy and citizenship. He wrote to his Virginia friend George Wythe in 1786, "I think by far the most important bill in our whole code, is that for the diffusion of knowledge among the people. No other sure foundation can be devised, for the preservation of freedom and happiness" (cited in Padover, 1953, p. 87).

My intention in this book is not to criticize anyone's religious convictions per se. There would be no reason to raise the issue of religious morality with regard to schools and literature were not the RR framing the debate in religious, particularly biblical, terms. Having done so, I believe their contentions must be met on the same level, using the same basic sources: the First Amendment, the writings of the Founding Fathers, and the Bible.

I agree with Thomas Jefferson, the arch defender of religious liberty who was attacked in his own day by conservative clergy as an "infidel," when he wrote in his only book *Notes on Virginia* (1781), "It does me no injury for my neighbor to say there are twenty gods, or no God. It neither picks my pocket nor breaks my leg" (cited in Larson, 1984, p. 321). However, when religion is used by critics as the basis for assaults on public education, teachers, and books, it makes a big difference. When successful, these attacks affect what can be offered to students, what reading materials can be purchased, and how teachers teach. The RR critics pick the pockets of taxpayers when schools are sued, and can "break the leg" of our long-standing commitment to a secular, public education through intimidation, threats, and school board takeovers.

If our schools are to continue into the 21st century, serving a pluralistic, multicultural, multireligious clientele, teaching children how to think, learn, and value themselves and others, we must courageously and wholeheartedly resist the efforts of those who wish to undermine public education. We must commit ourselves to the values of openness, equality, freedom of thought, speech, and inquiry—and most of all to the freedom to read.

I

THE CENSORSHIP DEBATE REGARDING PUBLIC SCHOOLS

1

The Debate Over Government and Religion

The First Amendment to the U. S. Constitution has a two-pronged section related to religion. The first part, called the Establishment Clause, states that "Congress shall make no laws respecting an establishment of religion." The second, the Free Exercise Clause, forbids creating laws that "prohibit the free exercise of religion."

A frequent claim of RR leaders is that the Founding Fathers used the Bible as the basis for our Republic, established America to be a Christian nation, and never intended for Christianity (defined as *born-again funda-mentalism*) to be separated from government. The just-cited clauses in the First Amendment, they say, mean only that government should not inter-fere with Christian churches.

ISSUE: IS AMERICA A CHRISTIAN NATION?

THE RELIGIOUS RIGHT'S CLAIM: America was established as a Chris-tian nation, based on biblical principles from which our country has drastically strayed. All government institutions, including public schools, should reflect that heritage only; other beliefs are heresy.

Shortly after his reelection as Speaker of the House in November 1996, Newt Gingrich said in his address to Congressional Republicans, "We have an obligation to reassert...that this nation comes from God, that it is in fact only successful when it is submissive to God's will" (cited in Boston, 1997, p. 4). At a Heritage Foundation dinner on December 3, 1996, he stated that those on the RR should "aggressively but calmly bring back to the public square the fact that we are a noble people motivated by a deep faith in God" (cited in Boston, 1997, p. 4). Although he denied advocating a national

3

religion, Gingrich has spoken at several Christian Coalition rallies, an organization that is striving to abolish the separation of church and state.

Televangelist Jerry Falwell is more direct. He wrote in *Listen, America!* (1980), "Our great nation was founded by godly men upon godly principles to be a Christian nation" (p. 29). The president of the ultra-right Rutherford Institute in Virginia stated that "the entire Constitution was written to promote a Christian order" (cited in Kramnick & Moore, 1996, p. 22). The statement, "The concept of a secular state was virtually non-existent in 1776 as well as in 1787, when the Constitution was written....The Constitution was designed to perpetuate a Christian order" (p. 20) can be found in *The Rebirth of America* (1986).

And who are the Christians? Only "the religious," as Pat Robertson (1993, p. 15), founder and head of the Christian Coalition put it, or the "people of faith" (1994) as the organization's former executive director Ralph Reed[1] repeatedly states, implying that those who profess religious beliefs different from the RR are not religious or a people of faith, even if they are actively involved in mainstream Christian denominations or other religious institutions.

On his televised "The 700 Club" program, January 14, 1991, Robertson said, "You say you're supposed to be nice to the Episcopalians and the Presbyterians and the Methodists and this, that, and the other thing. Nonsense! I don't have to be nice to the spirit of the Antichrist"; Hinduism he called "devil worship" (January 7, 1991), believing it to be tied to "New Age" philosophies which he also despises; Mormons may be nice people, he said, but they "are far from biblical truth" (July 4, 1995) and are going to burn in hell along with the "half of all adults who attend Protestant churches on a typical Sunday morning" (June 5, 1995) who are not "born-again" (cited in Boston, 1996b, pp. 149, 151, 153, 154).

Textbook critic Mel Gabler stated in an interview, "Roman Catholics do not teach the gospel, and are, therefore, not necessarily Christians" (cited in Martin, 1982, p. 151). Tim LaHaye called Catholicism a "false religion," saying that "Rome is more dangerous than no religion, because she substitutes religion for truth" (cited in Robinson, 1987, p. 1).

The Jewish faith is also denigrated by the RR. LaHaye stated, "Brilliant [Jewish] minds have all too frequently been devoted to philosophies that have proved harmful to mankind" (cited in Robinson, 1987, p. 1). Falwell pronounced that Jews are "spiritually blind" (cited in Bergstrom, 1985, p. 4), and Bailey Smith, former president of the Southern Baptist Convention, proclaimed that God Almighty "does not hear the prayers of the Jew....For how in the world can God hear the prayer of a man who says Jesus Christ is not the true Messiah? That is blasphemy" (cited in Finch, 1983, p. 67).

---

[1] Ralph Reed resigned this position in April 1997 to form a political organization, Century Strategies, to promote RR candidates for public office, including public school boards (*Architect*, 1997, p. 2).

John Wheeler, Jr., former editor of *Christian America*, whose bible-prophecy book about the "end times" was endorsed by LaHaye and Reed, wrote about "Satanic pedophilia" rites and practices among Catholic bishops and priests and warned that there is a "reasonable possibility" that the successor to Pope John Paul II could be a "corrupt pope—an apostate, Satanically empowered." He also labeled as "cults" such other denominations as the Mormon church, Christian Science, and Jehovah's Witnesses, stated that Islam "bears a strong demonic stamp," and called Buddhism "idol worship" and Hinduism the "oldest false religion in the world" (cited in *Ralph Reed endorsement*, 1996, p. 14).

COUNTERARGUMENT: America was not founded as a Christian nation but a secular one, in which all religions can flourish without government interference, none should dominate, and religion is not favored over nonreligion.

More than 250 distinct religions exist in the United States, with widely divergent views on the meaning of earthly life and the possibility of a hereafter. Martin E. Marty, professor of the history of modern Christianity at the University of Chicago, pointed out in his book *Religion and Republic: The American Circumstance* (1987) that one of the strongest American traditions from the beginning of our nation has been religious pluralism. "Nowhere before or elsewhere has there been variety on the scale experienced here, or such a widespread acceptance of the grounding of that diversity, or such celebration of its positive values. No foreign visitor fails to observe it" (pp. 34–35).

Constitutional law expert Leonard W. Levy wrote in *The Establishment Clause* (1986):

> Given the extraordinary religious diversity of our nation, the establishment clause functions to depoliticize religion; it thereby helps to defuse a potentially explosive situation....The establishment clause separates government and religion so that we can maintain civility between believers and unbelievers as well as among the several hundred denominations, sects, and cults that thrive in our nation, all sharing the commitment to liberty and equality that cements us together. (p. ix)

Even in Christianity, which is the majority but not the established religion in this country, there are many denominations that differ from each other considerably. And within each one the ministers and congregational members often interpret the scriptures and tenets of their church in diverse ways.

RR leaders frequently cite as proof of America's establishment as a Christian nation the use of religious terms by the Founding Fathers. Being savvy politicians as well as spiritual persons, our forefathers did use religious language in their public pronouncements. A close study of their private correspondence, however, reveals a different picture with regard to churches and dogma. For instance, Thomas Jefferson was vilified by contemporary clergy as a "howling atheist"[2] whose election to the presidency would be "a rebellion against God" (cited in Cunningham, 1987, pp. 225, 230). He was reared an Anglican, accepted deism, leaned toward Unitarianism, respected the moral principles but not the theology of Jesus, and rarely went to church (Adams, 1983). Creeds, Jefferson wrote in a letter to a minister, "have been the bane and ruin of the Christian Church" and "made of Christendom a slaughterhouse" (June 5, 1822, cited in Larson, 1984, pp. 330-331).

Wrote the ever-zealous defender of religious liberty James Madison, "Who does not see that the same authority which can establish Christianity, in exclusion of all other Religions, may establish with the same ease any particular sect of Christians, in exclusion of all other Sects?" (cited in Seldes, 1985, p. 261).

In *Creeds in Competition* (1958), Leo Pfeffer noted that when the United States was formed, religion was at a low ebb, with no more than 10% of the population affiliated with any church:

> Next to the Bible, the most widely read and widely discussed book was Tom Paine's scoffing attack on the Bible, *The Age of Reason*. Religious skepticism permeated the universities....None of the first seven Presidents...was formally affiliated with any church. The drafters of the Constitution of the United States studiously avoided all reference to God in their document. The treaty negotiated with Tripoli in 1797 squarely avowed that "the government of the United States of America is not, in any sense, founded on the Christian religion." (p. 29)

Steeped in humanism and science, the Founding Fathers expressed a belief in a universal Providence, the importance of reason to solve earthly problems, and the need for justice, freedom, and harmony. They found beauty and wisdom in the Bible, as well as in other books, but believed that ethical behavior was the highest good. As Jefferson wrote to a friend, "It is in our lives, and not from our words, that our religion must be read" (August 6, 1816, cited in Larson, 1984, p. 327).

ISSUE: THE SEPARATION OF CHURCH AND STATE

THE RELIGIOUS RIGHT'S CLAIM: The Founding Fathers never intended a complete separation of church and state, but only that the government should not interfere with the religious beliefs and practices of Christians.

---

[2]The Rev. Thomas Robbins, South Carolina, declared during the presidential campaign that he would not believe that God would "permit a howling atheist to sit at the head of this nation."

According to Pat Robertson, the church–state separation idea is a recent deception by "radical left" groups who are striving to keep those who espouse RR views in submission. "There is no such thing in the Constitution. It's a lie of the left, and we're not going to take it any more" (cited in Boston, 1996c, p.10). At the Christian Coalition's 1996 "Road to Victory" conference, Robertson accused the American Civil Liberties Union (ACLU) "of trying to snuff out religious values from our public square in the name of this so-called separation of church and state which they've made up" (cited in Conn, 1996a, p. 6).

Following Robertson's lead, U. S. Congressman Jeff Sessions of Alabama called church–state separation an "extra-constitutional doctrine" and said it is a "recent thing that is unhistorical and unconstitutional" (cited in Johnson, 1997, p. 8). In a book by David Barton, *The Myth of Separation* (1992), which is popular with the Coalition and other RR followers, the author declared that modern Supreme Court justices were the ones who created the church–state separation concept to hide the Christian basis of our nation. He claimed, "Today we would best understand the actual context of the First Amendment by saying, 'Congress shall make no law establishing one Christian denomination as the national denomination'" (p. 28). He also stated, "Whatever is not a religion is not protected" (p. 30). [See Barton's recent retractions under COUNTERARGUMENT].

The "myth of separation" has believers in high places. Supreme Court Chief Justice William Rehnquist, in a dissenting opinion in a 1985 case that ruled against government-sponsored school prayer, wrote, "The 'wall of separation between church and state' is a metaphor based on bad history, a metaphor which has proved useless as a guide to judging. It should be frankly and explicitly abandoned" (*Wallace v. Jaffree*, 1985, p. 76).

Robert Bork, a rejected candidate for appointment to the Supreme Court, declared at a 1995 Christian Coalition rally, "We know from history that the framers and the ratifiers of the First Amendment did not intend to enact Jefferson's rigid wall of separation between church and state. Yet the court has built the Establishment Clause on Jefferson's views, which were idiosyncratic at the time" (cited in Boston, 1995, p. 13).

COUNTERARGUMENT: Although the words *separation of church and state* **do not appear in the Constitution, the intent of the framers is clear from speeches, letters, and other documents.**

Refuting the claims of the RR about the myth of separation, Cornell University professors Isaac Kramnick and R. Laurence Moore, explained in detail in *The Godless Constitution* (1996) the origin of the "wall of separation" concept (chapters 3–5). The idea was conceived much earlier by a European philosopher and brought to America by the dissenter Roger Williams 100 years before the Constitution was written. President Thomas

Jefferson used it in a letter to a group of Baptists in Danbury, Connecticut, in 1802:

> Believing with you that religion is a matter which lies solely between man and his God...I contemplate with sovereign reverence that act of the whole American people which declared that their legislature should 'make no law respecting an establishment of religion, or prohibiting the free exercise thereof,' thus building a wall of separation between church and state. (Kramnick & Moore, 1996, p. 97)

In 1946 in one of the early religion and public school cases, Justice Hugo Black reiterated Jefferson's words, stating that "the clause against establishment of religion by law was intended to erect 'a wall of separation between Church and State'" (*Everson v. Board of Education*, p. 18). Earlier in the mid-1800s, when Protestantism reigned supreme in public schools, the Civil War general and president of the United States Ulysses S. Grant agreed wholeheartedly with Jefferson's separation concept: "Leave the matter of religion to the family altar, the church, and the private school, supported entirely by private contributions. Keep the church and state forever separate" (cited in Frymier et al., 1995, p. 11). President John F. Kennedy, the first Catholic in the White House, stated firmly at a Houston Ministerial Association meeting in 1960, "I believe in an America where the separation of church and state is absolute" (cited in Seldes, 1985, p. 225).

A more recent president, Jimmy Carter, whose Southern Baptist convictions strongly influence his life, supported the concept of separation in his book *Living Faith* (1996):

> Separation of church and state doesn't just protect religion from government meddling. It is also a positive good, encouraging Americans to support hundreds of varied and active religious denominations, worshiping God in churches, synagogues, mosques, and temples of every size and type. (p. 131)

Unable to give citations when challenged by Humanities Emeritus Professor Robert S. Alley, David Barton (see THE RELIGIOUS RIGHT'S CLAIM) admitted in summer 1996 that a number of statements related to Christianity and the Bible that he claimed in his book were made by the Founding Fathers and other prominent historical persons were fabricated. His group, Wallbuilders, published a sheet called "Questionable Quotes" that lists some of the bogus quotations and recommends that Barton's readers not use the statements in speeches, articles, and letters to the editor as had frequently been done (cited in Boston, 1996a, p. 13).

For example, a statement now labeled false that Barton attributed in his book to James Madison reads:

> We have staked the whole future of American civilization, not upon the power of government, far from it. We have staked the future of all of our

political institutions upon the capacity of each and all of us to govern ourselves, . . . according to the Ten Commandments of God. (Barton, 1992, p. 245)

Some other "questionable quotes" are:

George Washington: "It is impossible to rightly govern the world without God and the Bible" (Barton, p. 248).

Benjamin Franklin: "He who shall introduce into public affairs the principles of primitive Christianity will change the face of the world" (Barton, p. 249).

The "sources" Barton cited for these quotes were other right-wing publications.

ISSUE: THE "DECAY" OF PUBLIC EDUCATION

THE RELIGIOUS RIGHT'S CLAIM: When the Supreme Court justices ruled against prayer and Bible-reading in public schools in the early 1960s, they began the steady downhill slide into the godless, immoral, valueless abyss that passes for education today.

"Public education in America...is destroying democracy in America," claimed Pat Robertson (1993, p. 216). Public schools are in the "stranglehold" of the National Education Association, which "is not interested in education, but in power and money" (p. 226). The leaders of public education are "fanatical ideologues" who are "not sane," continued Robertson. "They are a group of ideological extremists who are so fixated with their illogical educational theories that they have lost touch with reality" and their "crackpot theories are fast destroying not only the public school system but an entire generation of our young" (pp. 215–216).

In his book *The New World Order* (1991) Robertson described what has brought about, in his mind, this "decadence" of today's public schools and society:

The Supreme Court of the supposedly Christian United States guaranteed the moral collapse of this nation when it forbade children in the public schools to pray to the God of Jacob, to learn of His moral law or even view in their classrooms the heart of the law, the Ten Commandments, which children must obey for their own good or disobey at their peril. (p. 233)

In a February 1995 speech at William and Mary College in Virginia, Robertson equated the school prayer ruling with the crime of rape, saying it was "a rape of our nation's religious heritage, our national morality. . . .

Especially, a rape of our governing document, the United States Constitution" (cited in Boston, 1996b, p. 169).

A decade earlier, Jerry Falwell (1983) wrote, "I am forced to believe that the decay of the public school system accelerated into a downward spiral when prayer and Bible reading were removed by the U.S. Supreme Court" (p. 8). Ralph Reed (1994) proclaimed that "children are denied the right to pray in public schools" (p. 41). President Ronald Reagan said in his February 5, 1986, State of the Union message, "We must give back to our children their lost right to acknowledge God in their classrooms." Senator Jesse Helms blamed the 1962 school prayer decision for bringing into public schools not only drugs but "pornography, crime, and fornication," saying that "a greater crime against our children could hardly be conceived" (cited in Falwell, 1980, p. 222). And despite the First Amendment, Jack Kemp, the 1996 Republican vice-presidential candidate, stated that the Ten Commandments should be posted in every school in America (cited in Conn, 1996c, p. 5).

COUNTERARGUMENT: Children can pray any time, silently and voluntarily as the Bible recommends (Matt. 6:7, "When thou prayest, enter into thy closet"), and the Bible may be studied academically in public schools. The Supreme Court ruled only that government-sponsored prayer and Bible-reading as religious exercises were a violation of the neutrality clause of the First Amendment.

Despite the RR's assertion that the Founding Fathers did not intend for government to be separated from religion, the wall of separation phrase has been used repeatedly by the courts as the basis for determining what is legal and illegal with regard to such things as school prayer, Bible reading, posting the Ten Commandments, singing religious music, and displaying Christian symbols during Christmas and Easter holidays in public schools. The first person to devise a plan for 3 years of free public-supported education in America (for White children) was Thomas Jefferson in Virginia. It was not initially passed by the state legislature, but became the prototype for public education in other states, beginning with Massachusetts and Connecticut. Two important features of this plan were to teach the values of the newly formed republic and to be secular; that is, to be religiously neutral.

Instead "of putting the Bible and Testament into the hands of children at an age when their judgments are not sufficiently matured for religious inquiries," wrote Jefferson, "their memories may here be stored with the most useful facts from Grecian, Roman, European and American history" (cited in Larson, 1984, p. 252). Furthermore, those appointed to oversee these schools should not be "ministers of the gospel of any denomination" (cited in Larson, p. 253). However, as the schools grew, they became decidedly Christian and Protestant. Until the 1962 and 1963 Supreme Court decisions,[3] morning worship typically began with teacher or student-led prayer and Bible reading. RR believers look enviably back on those days when Protestantism predominated. Or even farther back to colonial days in New England when Puritanism ruled and followers of other faiths, such as Baptists, Quakers, Catholics, and Jews, were banned from the colony or brutally persecuted.

The *Engel* and *Schempp* rulings against state-sponsored prayer and Bible reading in public schools, however, did not steal from children their right to acknowledge God, but merely reinforced the First Amendment's neutrality clause. These were religious exercises and thus constituted an establishment of religion, which infringed on children who came from families with different or no religious beliefs.

Furthermore, Justice Tom Clark stated clearly in *Abington v. Schempp* (1963) that the Bible could and should be read in classrooms as part of students' academic education:

> It certainly may be said the Bible is worthy of study for its literary and historic qualities. Nothing we have said here indicates that such study of the Bible or of religion, when presented objectively as part of a secular program of education, may not be effected consistently with the First Amendment. (p. 860)

Although the *wall* concept has been the legal interpretation of the First Amendment for more than 200 years, a complete separation of religion and government is probably an impossibility. Martin Marty (1987) noted that religion is not confined to formal institutions, but is "unmistakably and increasingly diffused throughout the culture" (p. 11). The problem for courts and public institutions, then, becomes how broadly is religion to be defined and "where does religion *stop?*" (p. 21). The Court has also recognized that religion is such an integral part of society that it cannot be totally removed from state functions. Thus, in *Lemon v. Kurtzman* (1971), the "Lemon test" was created as a means of clarifying the issue (a test the RR strongly opposes). The Justices established three criteria to evaluate the legality of an activity in such places as public schools:

- it must be secular in nature
- it must neither advance nor prohibit religion
- there must be no "excessive entanglement" of government and religion. (p. 755)

---

[3]In the *Engel v. Vitale* case (1962), the Supreme Court found unconstitutional the New York Regents "nondenominational" prayer that was recommended to be said each morning in every public school in the state. The following year, in *Abington v. Schempp; Murray v. Curlett* (1963), Bible reading as a morning exercise was also ruled a violation of the First Amendment's clause forbidding the establishment of a religion.

The latter, however, implies that some entanglement is unavoidable and acceptable. The questions for society and state-supported schools are: what kind and how much?

Charles Haynes, a 1996 visiting scholar at the Freedom Forum First Amendment Center, Vanderbilt University, advocated having academic studies on the Bible and world religions in public schools. The purpose would not be to promote any particular faith or to proselytize, but to expose students to the cultural and intellectual aspects of many religions: "Students who know how humankind has struggled with the great religious questions are not so vulnerable to the nonsense and dangerous ideas spouted by certain groups and movements" (cited in Reunzel, 1996, p. 33).

Agreeing with this idea is Warren Nord, director of the Program in the Humanities and Human Values at the University of North Carolina, Chapel Hill, and author of *Religion and American Education* (1996): "One of the most dangerous assumptions educators make is that we should teach our idea of truth. But being truly well-educated means knowing alternatives to your idea of truth" (cited in Reunzel, p. 33).

However, reading the Bible as part of a secular program of education, studying the doctrines and practices of world religions, and being confronted with other concepts of truth is to the RR worse than avoiding religion altogether, for this opens the door to biblical scholarship, historical and literary studies, archeological findings, comparisons with "pagan" religions, and various interpretations of scriptural passages.

Contrary to the statements of RR leaders, government schools are not antagonistic to religious beliefs, but must draw a line between an academic study of an important part of our culture and an unconstitutional preference of one faith over others, or of religion over nonbelief. Thus, reading the Ten Commandments and comparing them with similar tenets in other religions would be a legitimate lesson; posting the Commandments in every classroom would be a promotion of the Judeo-Christian faith and a violation of the First Amendment.

A discussion of religion is legal in any class where it is integral to the subject. For instance, many historical topics, from medievalism to Martin Luther to the Mayflower Compact, cannot be understood without investigating the religious underpinnings. Novels, short stories, and poetry are especially laden with religious elements, including biblical and other scriptural references from a variety of faiths.

In August 1995, the U.S. Department of Education disseminated to every school district in America a statement of principles concerning "the extent to which religious expression and activity are permitted in public schools." In the introduction, President Bill Clinton stated:

> Nothing in the First Amendment converts our public schools into religion-free zones, or requires all religious expression to be left behind at the

schoolhouse door. While the government may not use schools to coerce the consciences of our students, or to convey official endorsement of religion, the public schools also may not discriminate against private religious expression during the school day....Religion is too important in our history and our heritage for us to keep it out of our schools.[4] (Riley, 1995, p. 1).

Thus, in addition to learning about religion in academic classes, students can practice their faith in a variety of ways that do not interfere with the rights of others. They can pray silently, read the Bible on their own time, request alternate books that are compatible with their beliefs, and express their religious convictions whenever it is appropriate for such discussions.

Teachers, however, have a sometimes difficult task. They must walk a narrow path between promoting a common core of democratic values, discussed in the next chapter, and those values that reflect only the beliefs of specific religious groups. They must determine what constitutes an academic study, what becomes indoctrination into a particular faith, what is discrimination against private religious expression or nonreligious belief, and what is a valid, even necessary, means of educating students in a democratic society.

---

[4]A free copy of the principles can be obtained from the U. S. Department of Education, Washington, DC.

2

The Debate Over Humanism
and Democracy

A fairly new idea has entered the fray over censorship and public schools and has proved to be an effective challenge. RR leaders claim that schools teach a "liberal religion" or "the religion of secular humanism" and forbid conservative Christians from practicing theirs, thus violating both segments of the First Amendment's religion clause (see chapter 1). This argument, which sounds plausible and has supporters among high government officials, was launched in the 1974 Kanawha County episode (see the Introduction) when a petition was drawn up by protestors that said the following:

> Inasmuch as it has been held unconstitutional for a tax-supported school to promote religious belief, we hold that it is equally unconstitutional to promote religious disbelief. Further, since the denial of supernatural forces is in itself a form of religion, the promotion of agnosticism or nihilism must also be unconstitutional. (cited in Hefley, 1977, p. 163–164)

Because RR extremists are convinced that everything is religious in nature, and all beliefs other than theirs are false and dangerous, every school book, program, and activity either promotes the RR dogma or promotes the devil's. There is no in-between. What most people consider merely secular, the RR perceives to be the Satan-inspired "religion of secular humanism."

Currently, RR leaders maintain that the courts have moved from "neutrality to hostility towards religion" (Reed, 1994, p. 78). By drastically distorting the concept of secular humanism, they have found a way to use the First Amendment to attack schools and teachers and impose their own religious views on public education. The RR defines humanism in diabolical ways, insists that it is a religion, and that it is being taught in public schools while other beliefs are forbidden, especially theirs. Thus, govern-

14

ment schools are in their view violating the Constitution by illegally forcing on all students the amoral religion of secular humanism (or plain humanism) and forbidding RR children from practicing their faith in the classroom.

According to Texas public-school critics, Norma and Mel Gabler (1985):

> The "Free Exercise" clause of the First Amendment is violated when evolution, situation ethics, and other humanistic doctrines are foisted on students by subtle coercion, indoctrination, or peer pressure from other indoctrinated students. . . . Humanists have no right to force their religious views on students under the guise of "neutral" education. (p. 166)

Similar statements are found in the writings, speeches, and letters of RR proponents across the land.

ISSUE: WHAT IS SECULAR HUMANISM?

THE RELIGIOUS RIGHT'S CLAIM: The religion of secular humanism, which has taken over public education and our society, is destroying our children and our nation's future. Christians are daily being persecuted by the government, the courts, the media, and the schools.

In his book *Answers* (1984), Pat Robertson stated that the public school curriculum indoctrinates students with humanism, which is "an attempt to wean children away from biblical Christianity" (p. 192). On a "700 Club" broadcast in 1992 he exclaimed that "children are being beat up by humanist teachers and misguided educators all over America" (cited in Boston, 1996b, p. 211).

Tim LaHaye declared that "*academic freedom* means that humanists and other atheists are free to teach their atheistic beliefs, but Christians may not teach theirs. Consequently atheism has become the official doctrine of public education" (1982, p. 91). The schools label it "democracy," he said, "but they mean humanism, in all its...amoral depravity," which he believed to be "the most serious threat to our nation in its entire history" (1980, pp. 142, 187).

Jerry Falwell called secular humanism the "cult of atheism" and said that because of the "gurus of progressive education" and the wrongheaded decisions of liberal courts, public school teachers "cannot teach values, they dare not mention the existence of God, and actual discipline is out of the question....It is no longer possible to point to the religious heritage of this country in America's public schools" (1992, pp. 78–79).

When running for the 1996 presidential nomination, Patrick Buchanan said at a rally, "We see a cultural war going on for the soul of America. We see the God of the Bible expelled from our public schools and replaced by all the false gods of secular humanism. Easter is out, but we can celebrate Earth Day. We can now worship dirt" (cited in Bullough, 1996, p. 11).

RR proponents see themselves as being horribly mistreated by this unconstitutional, ungodly "establishment" of a "secular religion" in public schools. In the "atheistic philosophy" of secular humanism, according to Falwell (1992), "nothing is sacred. Every person can choose his or her own values and all choices are equal, with one notable exception: The only ones deemed unacceptable are traditional Christian values. The open-minded secular humanists have no place in their philosophy for the Christian world view" (p. 78).

Robertson compared the "plight" of the RR to the victims of the Nazi Holocaust, slavery, and other atrocities. He railed on the air against humanist leaders and educators who "victimize" those of the RR:

> Just like what Nazi Germany did to the Jews, so liberal America is now doing to the evangelical Christians. It's no different....the worst bigotry directed toward any group in America today. More terrible than anything suffered by any minority in our history. (Cantor, 1994, p. 4)

In *Politically Incorrect* (1994), Ralph Reed claimed, "Today the First Amendment has been twisted into a weapon that billy-clubs people of faith into submission and silence. The Bible...is now treated as contraband. Our legal and political culture has created a bias in the law that borders on censorship against reading, displaying, or quoting the Bible" (p. 43).

LaHaye (1992) saw this humanist "destruction" of schools and society as a "satanically-inspired, centuries old conspiracy to use government, education, and media to destroy every vestige of Christianity within our society and establish a new world order" (p. 136). Robertson (1993) laid the blame on organizations such as the American Civil Liberties Union and People For the American Way that have been "waging a vicious war on our traditional values and the free expression of our religious beliefs" (p. 119).

According to a survey done by the American Bible Society, 90% of Americans own a Bible and 55% attend church at least once a week (a figure much higher than most Western nations), and a World Values Survey reported that 82% of Americans consider themselves religious (cited in *Constitutional amendment*, 1995, p. 13). Yet, Robertson (1993) claimed that the "liberal left" has "virtually stripped this nation of any visible evidence of faith or belief in God" (p. 119).

How does the RR define *humanism*? Falwell (1980) said in *Listen, America!* that "man, rather than God, has been placed at the center of all things. . . . When mankind absolves his Christian base, he loses respect for human life" (pp. 65, 67). Over the years Falwell has charged that humanism advocates pornography, prostitution, infanticide, suicide, gambling, and drug use—and promotes these in the public schools.

Believing this to be true, Rich Scarborough, minister of the 1,400-member First Baptist Church in Pearland, Texas, proclaimed, "It's time for a David to stand up to the Goliath of secular humanism in America and cut off the head of the wicked giant" (cited in Conn, 1996b, p. 12). The Gablers, whose arguments in Texas against many textbooks have caused major publishers to alter what children across the nation are able to read, have made plain their reasons for opposing humanism: "[It] is a religion with an anti-biblical, anti-God bent. It worships the creature instead of the Creator" and "puts man, not God, at the center of all" (1985, pp. 42, 44). The humanists' ultimate aim, claimed the Gablers, "is to phase out traditional marriage and family relationships" (p. 160).

COUNTERARGUMENT: Humanism has a long, respected history, is not the vile, diabolical plot to destroy children that the RR claims, and is a philosophy, not a religion. In truth, it is the basis for American democracy and a legitimate foundation of public education.

Despite their desires, even RR leaders today sometimes admit that "reverting all schools back to Christ" is probably forbidden by the Constitution and especially by numerous Supreme Court decisions. Thus, in recent years they have attempted to inject right-wing extremist views into public school curriculums by means of the First Amendment's freedom of religion clause. Rather than claiming, as they once did, that schools are hostile to all religious beliefs, they now assert that schools are illegally teaching the "established religion" of humanism, more often called secular humanism.

That is a clever argument, except that the term, as they define it, is not the philosophy of humanism that the rest of the world knows. Instead it consists of everything those on the far right despise—feminism, open-ended discussions, free inquiry, literature, sex and drug education, critical thinking, creativity, and worst of all New Age beliefs and practices that, in their minds, advocate wizardry, witchcraft, and the occult. Public school educators of all faiths, they claim, either willingly or by force are feeding children poisons that will destroy their minds and souls.

To prove that humanism is a religion, RR followers point to a footnote in a 1961 Supreme Court decision, *Torcaso v. Watkins* that struck down a Maryland requirement that all state officers profess a belief in God, ruling it unconstitutional to "impose requirements which aid all religions as against non-believers" (6 L. Ed. 2d, p. 987). In footnote 11 Justice Black listed Secular Humanism along with Buddhism, Taoism, and Ethical Culture as examples of religions "which do not teach what would generally be considered a belief in the existence of God" (6 L Ed, p. 987).

Although the term *secular humanism* was coined earlier[1] and used as the name for a small organization in Northern California, its popular usage

---

[1]William Safire (1986) reported that the first citation of *secular humanism* in Merriam-Webster's files was from a religious work in 1933 by William G. Peck called *The Social Implications of the Oxford Movement*, in which secular humanism was opposed to Catholicism.

came from the above case, after lawyer Leo Pfeffer argued for the plaintiff Torcaso. In writing the majority opinion, Justice Hugo Black lifted the phrase *Secular Humanism* from Pfeffer's book *Creeds in Competition* (1958) and included it in the footnote as an example of a nondeistic religion.

In his book Pfeffer stated that he was using secular humanism (spelled with lowercase letters) "not to mean a consciously non-theistic movement, but merely the influence of those unaffiliated with organized religion and concerned with human values" (footnote, p. 29). In no way did the term secular humanism as used by Pfeffer imply the Satan-inspired conspiracy the RR disparages.

Religion historian Martin Marty asserted in *Religion and Republic* (1987) that the secular humanism the RR decries is not the small minority of those who actually profess beliefs in this philosophy, but is a cover for the pluralism in our country that the RR finds so menacing. A multiplicity of beliefs, he wrote "is unappealing to those who are losing their status as dominators of a culture. Pluralism appears as a code word for a conspiracy that would prevent new aspirants to power from gaining it" (p. 5). Because being against pluralism is today not a politically correct posture, the term secular humanism serves in its place to alarm those who are afraid their right-wing views are being rejected by the majority of Americans.

Agreeing with this sentiment, Daniel Keyes, author of *Flowers for Algernon*, an oft-challenged story, said the following:

> It seems to me that they are trying to create a bogus religion out of two neutral words. What they are really doing is creating a straw man. What we are seeing is a classic technique of propagandists—the technique of attaching a false label to something you don't believe in and then using that label as a weapon. The label becomes a rallying cry, and secular humanism has become a rallying cry for the fundamentalists. The other propagandist technique that they're using is repeating their charge over and over again. They hope that if they say that secular humanism is a religion often enough it will make it so. McCarthy used similar tactics. (cited in West, 1988, p. 84)

Still, the argument that the state is imposing a secular religion (an oxymoron) on students and banning RR views poses a problem for schools in their attempt to be neutral with regard to all religions and with nonbelief. One of the areas most likely to engender a clash of values, as we shall see, is the literature read in classrooms and found in school libraries.

What exactly is humanism? The philosophy emerged in the 14th century in Italy and spread to the rest of Europe in what is known as the Renaissance, or awakening. Although it was a revolt against the other-worldliness of Medieval Christianity and the restriction of knowledge, it initially grew within the church itself. Christian scholars turned their focus from preparing for life after death to living a full life on earth. They took seriously Psalm 8:4, "What is man that thou art mindful of him? Yet thou has made him little less than God, and dost crown him with glory and honor." To encourage and praise human achievement and to work toward improving earthly life was to glorify the Creator. Those who in our day call themselves humanists are the best source for understanding what it entails. According to Corliss Lamont (1982), a leading proponent of humanism, in the New Testament Jesus is portrayed as raising "his voice again and again on behalf of broad Humanist ideals such as social equality, the development of altruism, the brotherhood of man, and peace on earth" (p. 51).

The roots of humanism lie not only in the Bible, but in Confucianism, Buddhism, and other great religions. The tradition, as described by Lamont (1982) in *The Philosophy of Humanism*, "holds as its highest goal the this-worldly happiness, freedom, and progress—economic, cultural, and ethical—of all mankind, irrespective of nation, race, or religion" (pp. 256–257). It assumes that people have some control over their environment and destinies and are not puppets dangled by the strings of a capricious, vengeful God.

Humanism is a declaration that human beings have created earthly problems and have the responsibility and capability of solving them by their own efforts. Although some humanists and theists may disagree, humanism in my opinion is not a religion, but an approach to the world, a set of values and a way of thinking that is compatible with any religion or nonreligion that asserts that humans have the capacity to reason and should use their minds for the good of others and themselves.

Humanists do not believe that anything goes, that there is no right and wrong, but rather that ethical standards are formed by human experience. They find guidance in many sources, including the Bible. Humanists strive for such common moral values as honesty, responsibility, integrity, altruism, and kindness. They believe in promoting moral development in children and nourishing compassion as well as reason.

Well-versed in the humanism that grew out of the Enlightenment period, especially the writings of John Locke, our country's forefathers such as Paine, Jefferson, Madison, and Franklin were committed to establishing a free society where religions of all types could flourish, none would wield power over others, and no one would be forced to follow any belief or pay taxes for any church. They also championed diversity of opinion, a scientific approach to knowledge, freedom of inquiry and expression, and the good of the community. In *The Establishment Clause* (1986), Leonard Levy wrote that "rationalists, Unitarians, and Deists, like Benjamin Franklin and Thomas Jefferson" were the "'secular humanists' of their time" (p. xi).

Lamont (1982) defined 20th-century humanism as a "philosophy of joyous service for the greater good of all humanity in this natural world and advocating the methods of reason, science, and democracy" (p. 12).

The humanist ethic, he added, "urges the development of those basic impulses of love, friendliness, and cooperation that impel a person to consider constantly the good of the group and to find his own happiness in working for the happiness of all" (p. 249).

Humanists may or may not seek supernatural inspiration through prayer, meditation, and religious Scriptures. Some call themselves secular, and others ground their humanistic beliefs in a chosen faith. For example, Marquette University, a Jesuit institution in Milwaukee, Wisconsin, includes in its brochures a statement of its commitment to "Christian Humanism" and requires of all students an academic study of core disciplines in what for centuries constituted a liberal education.

Thus the secular humanism that is taught in schools encourages students to think for themselves, explore new ideas and knowledge, read about other cultures, develop their imagination and creative talents, and live in harmony with others. It does not negate religion or teach atheism, but promotes the democratic ideal of freedom of thought, expression, and inquiry. It attempts to instill morality in children, not by blind obedience but through interacting with others, reasoning from experience, and reading and discussing worthwhile books.

Responding to the distortions of humanistic principles by the Gablers, whom he interviewed, journalist William Martin (1982) expressed well the true essence of humanism and why it is, and should continue to be, the underlying philosophy of our public schools:

> In education, this humanistic approach does not seek to ply children with pot, pills, pornography, and polymorphous perversity. Rather it strives to instill in them habits of mind and qualities of spirit that will include a love for knowledge, a depth and breadth of understanding, an ability to think well and critically for themselves, a belief in their essential worthiness and in that of others, and a desire and ability to work for the common good. (p. 268)

Major aims of humanistic education are not only to promote a love for learning and an intellectual approach to life, but to build a compassionate, just, and free society that promotes the welfare of individuals as well as the community.

ISSUE: HUMANISM AND DEMOCRACY

THE RELIGIOUS RIGHT'S CLAIM: Humanism is the opposite of democracy and will be its destruction.

Pat Robertson (1993) claimed that public education is "about controlling the minds and hearts of the young," and the "landmarks and important fundamentals of history, literature, language, science, mathematics, and the arts" are "rarely if ever covered" in modern textbooks (pp. 236–238).

The RR's arch enemy in education, the demonic father who they believe started school's slide into Satanism, is the renowned philosopher and educator John Dewey. Said Robertson (1991), "Since Dewey began his notorious career at Columbia, twisting and shaping the values and behaviors of American scholars and teachers, the secular establishment has been patiently and persistently dismantling America's inherited value system and its ethical foundations" (p. 164).

These right-wing extremists claim, however, that they do not want to make our nation a theocracy, are not trying to impose their beliefs on the rest of society or on public schools. All they want is a "place at the table in the conversation we call democracy" (Reed, 1994, p. 24). In replying to the frequently used phrase that education should be a *marketplace of ideas*, RR proponents argue that humanists permit all ideas in the classroom except those of "traditional Christian viewpoints and values," and that is not democratic.

The Gablers have said that they are not against intellectual inquiry and discussion. "We welcome discussion—when the students are given adequate information on *both sides*. We want balance. We simply object to one-sided indoctrination to suit the ideology of the educational establishment" (1985, p. 60). Nor are they against students learning about nonbiblical religions, but object to the indoctrination of the tenets of these religions and the "textbooks being used as channels for attacks on biblical beliefs and Judeo-Christian morals" (p. 39).

COUNTERARGUMENT: Humanism and democracy are not synonymous, but are compatible and contain many of the same elements.

The biggest problem democracy has, said the Christian theologian Reinhold Niebuhr (1960), is how to integrate the various subordinate groups—ethnic, religious, economic—into a community so that the welfare and harmony of the whole is enhanced and not destroyed (p. 124). This is also the biggest problem for public schools. Today, more than ever before, the student population is widely diverse racially, religiously, and culturally. Teachers must neither tread on the belief system of various religious groups nor allow any to set up barriers that limit what other people's children may do, explore, or read. Major problems arise, however, when the convictions of a particular group run counter to the tenets of democracy and threaten the freedom of others. This is the dilemma we explore later in relation to literature commonly taught in public high schools.

Right-wing extremists are not the only ones who seek to have their opinions prevail in schools, but because they have launched a frontal, debilitating attack on public education, using their religious convictions as the basis for the assault, they are the ones to be examined in this debate over censorship. What are some of the major differences between the RR beliefs and democratic principles?

First of all, democracy seeks truth by starting with questions rather than answers, subjects all knowledge to continual evaluation, and encourages skepticism. Although sociologists Robert Bellah (1974) and Will Herberg (1974) have proposed a "civil religion" theory that claims Americans "worship" the Founding Fathers, view the Constitution and other documents as the political "bible," and sing hymns glorifying our country, other scholars do not perceive democracy as a religion, nor as something opposed to most faiths. It does not rest on church dogma, religious scriptures, or moral absolutes for guidance, but leaves citizens free to believe as they wish as long as their actions do not infringe on the liberty of others.

Daniel Maguire, professor of ethics at Marquette University, pointed out that all patriotism has a religious component. "It comes from the period where we worshiped our tribes and conjured up national gods for them," but added that it is the deifying of nations that is unhealthy and can lead to such atrocities as Nazism. "Hitler's troops," he said, "wore *Gott mit uns* on their buckles" (Personal communication, December 1996).

In his monumental book, *Puritanism and Democracy* (1944), historian Ralph Barton Perry said that democracy is not in itself a religion but "a zealous devotion to a moral cause" (p. 623). Like humanism, democracy focuses on humans but does not worship them or equate them with a Supreme Being. On the other hand, a certain kind of religion, said Reinhold Niebuhr, is "so frequently a source of confusion in political life and so frequently dangerous to democracy, precisely because it introduces absolutes into the realm of relative values" (cited in Frohnmayer, 1994, p. 57). Niebuhr (1960) further stated, "Some of the greatest perils of democracy arise from the fanaticism of moral idealists who are not conscious of the corrupting self-interest in their professional ideals" (p. 151).

Second, democracy seeks consensus rather than conformity. Said Thomas Jefferson, "Is uniformity of opinion desirable? No more than of face and stature" (Padover, 1953, p. 110). Errors cease to be dangerous when argument and debate are left free to contradict them. Decisions are reached by dialog, open discussions, and persuasion, and not by adherence to preset, absolute standards demanded by the RR. It also supports access to knowledge. Citizens are encouraged to read extensively, contemplate a variety of opinions, and critically evaluate information. New ideas are welcomed and encouraged, rather than assailed and forbidden, and a bright future rather than an idealized past is a source of inspiration and encouragement.

From the 1930s to the 1950s, often cited by the RR as the *good old days* of American education, the progressive educator John Dewey (1939) feared, even then, the influence of right-wing religious thought on American society. "The historic influence of religions has often been to magnify doctrines that are not subject to critical inquiry and test. Their cumulative effect in producing habits of mind at odds with the attitudes required for maintenance of democracy is probably much greater than is usually recognized" (p. 151). Expanding on this belief, in a book sponsored by the Freedom Forum First Amendment Center at Vanderbilt University, visiting scholar John Frohnmayer (1994) explained that democracy "is improvisation. It proceeds on the assumption that no one knows enough to make irrevocable decisions, so that everything is in a continual state of flux. It puts aside the desire to be secure in favor of the privilege to be free" (p. 14).

In contrast, those on the extreme right, in their quest for safety and salvation, exhibit evidence of an excessive fear of change, of new knowledge, of examining information, ideas, and values, and of a future different from their real or imagined past where all was certain and secure. They appear to be desperately trying to preserve an old way of life for themselves and their families that is being demolished by the forces of modernism, which they believe to be the work of the devil.

A primary target of their energies is the public school, the institution most accessible and economically vulnerable to threatening challenges. If successful in getting removed from schools all materials, activities, and programs that differ from what they experienced as a child or that offer alternatives to what they want students to learn and believe, RR parents can perhaps forestall the inevitability of change and reduce their offspring's exposure to new knowledge, new concepts, and other "errors" or "harmful influences." This assumes, of course, that the children are not being exposed to other influences such as television, movies, magazines, video games, and peers.

However, our democracy established by the U.S. Constitution provides no protection from ideas that a person finds disagreeable or false, that offend anyone's religious or philosophical beliefs. Just the opposite. As Oliver Wendell Holmes stated in his famous dissenting opinion, "If there is any principle of the Constitution that more imperatively calls for attachment than any other, it is the principle of free thought—not free for those who agree with us but freedom for the thought that we hate" (dissent, *U.S. v. Schwimmer*, 1928, pp. 654-655).

RR leaders maintain that it is not they but liberal teachers who are unconstitutionally squelching the free thought of ideas they hate—the beliefs of right-wing fundamentalists. Although the expression has become trite, government schools do have an obligation to be a marketplace of ideas, where students are purposefully exposed to current information, historical scholarship, quality literature, and a variety of thoughts on a range of subjects. These thoughts should include the viewpoints of those on the RR along with many others, because they will continue to be voiced in the future. Students, however, should not be told to blindly accept whatever they read or hear, but to question, argue, and make critical judgments about the concepts of democracy and humanism, RR beliefs, and any other ideas. Wrote Thomas Jefferson to his nephew in 1787, "Question with boldness even the existence of God; because, if there be one, he must more approve of the homage of reason, than that of blindfolded fear" (cited in Larson, 1984, p. 332).

Questioning or criticizing their beliefs, especially their view of God, of course, is what RR proponents cannot tolerate. However, they vigorously and sometimes viciously attack everyone else's. They want other people's children as well as their own to hear only their views, the truth as they perceive it. If RR parents wish their children to know only one viewpoint and read only RR-approved materials, then they have the option of private institutions or homeschooling. They do not, however, have the right to limit the education of all other children whose parents do not share their extremist beliefs.

Because freedom is "imprecise, inefficient, ambiguous, and often annoying," said Frohnmayer (1994), those who prefer order and absolutes frequently resort to censorship to ensure the kind of insulated security they seek for themselves and their children. Censorship, he maintained "is an issue of control, of power over what others will or will not have the opportunity to experience" (pp. 46–47).

The reason censorship is so difficult to fight, said Robert Cormier (1994), whose books for young adults are often prime targets, is that it is

> the act of sincere, sometimes desperate people who are frightened by the world they live in and in which they are bringing up their children. They are trying to do the impossible, to shield their children from this world, to control what they see and do, what they learn....Instead of preparing them to meet that world, they want them to avert their eyes and remain in impossible exclusion (p. 71).

Public education is in grave danger from the attacks of RR extremists. The battle lines are clearly drawn, and the fight to teach democracy in our schools versus sectarianism will likely be hard fought and bruising. RR proponents are shrewd, well-organized, and powerful. Teachers, administrators, parents, and other concerned citizens who believe with Thomas Jefferson that a humanistic, liberal education is the foundation of a free society must rally their forces and defend the right of children to learn, to inquire, to read, to work together, and to speak and write their thoughts without the debilitating limits set by the ultraconservatives on the RR.

3

The Debate Over the Purpose
of Teaching Literature

Many reasons exist for choosing materials for classroom reading or school libraries, such as the literary value of the works, the maturity and reading ability of the students, the time available for teaching a novel, the achievement of a balance between contemporary books and classics, and the integration of writings by women and multicultural authors into the traditional canon.

Because only a handful of books can be selected out of hundreds of possibilities, compelling reasons must exist for choosing certain works over others. One of those, I believe, should be the moral value. First, teachers have characteristically shied away from selecting or defending books from a moral point of view. They are usually taught in college to evaluate the literary worth, so that is where they feel more secure. Second, they wish to stay neutral and not get involved in disputes over moral or religious issues. Third, when attacked by right-wing critics for teaching *immoral* books, they have a natural desire to elevate the discussion to a more objective, less emotional, plane.

According to the RR, public schools, which once reinforced the values of the majority of Americans, no longer teach any values, or are teaching the values of relativism and situational ethics, which will destroy our children. The primary job of the school, said Ralph Reed (1994), who at the time was executive director of the Christian Coalition:

> is to reinforce the basic values taught at home, not experiment with alternative value systems (p. 70). . .Children should be taught right from wrong. They are moral creatures, and they should be treated as such . . .and the rights of parents to mold and shape the souls of their children should be respected. (p. 257)

Parents of all persuasions, not just the RR, are concerned about their children learning right from wrong, about developing good characters.

They recognize that books are moral influencers. All parents have the right to question a school's or teacher's selection of books and to raise objections about either the literary quality or moral content. Teachers need to be ready and willing, therefore, to defend their book choices on the basis of moral values as well as other criteria.

ISSUE: WHY TEACH LITERATURE?

THE RELIGIOUS RIGHT'S CLAIM: The primary—in fact the only—reason for teaching literature in school is to reinforce the values that are taught in the home. Any book that does not have a religiously moral theme and that does not support Judeo-Christian values has no place in the classroom.

Because America was founded as a Christian nation, and only *people of faith* (read far-right fundamentalist Christians) are truly Christian, only books they approve should be allowed in public school classrooms and libraries, say RR critics. Teachers who assign humanistic books are destroying not only the minds and morals of America's youth, but the future of our country.

The RR contends further that until persons are born again, their natural propensity is toward evil. Thus, if any people in a story act in foolish or disturbing ways, no matter what the context or outcome, teenage readers will want to emulate them. If even a minor character or a *bad guy* uses profanity, talks about sex or engages in it, takes drugs, or defies an authority figure, adolescent readers will be attracted to that behavior and do likewise. Books given to students must entirely promote the RR value system or they will be doing the work of Satan.

An example of RR attacks on immoral books occurred in Panama City, Florida, in 1987. Sixty books were ordered removed by the school superintendent. Only 2 years earlier the Mowat Middle School had been designated a Center of Excellence by the National Council of Teachers of English for its literature program. The banned titles included such popular works as *The Call of the Wild, Of Mice and Men, Animal Farm, Fahrenheit 451, A Separate Peace, The Red Badge of Courage, Macbeth, King Lear,* and *Oedipus the King.* Eventually all were reinstated, except for Robert Cormier's *I Am the Cheese,* because of its "negative attitude toward government," and Farley Mowat's *Never Cry Wolf,* a story about tracking wolves in the Arctic, because of several mild expletives (Hentoff, 1987).

RR leaders claim that they are not censors. They are not against assigning students good books. What they desire are simply stories that exalt "honesty, virtue, decency, family, and sexual morality. All we want is good literature with a wholesome purpose" (Gabler & Gabler, 1985, p. 95).

COUNTERARGUMENT: A primary reason for teaching literature is to enlarge the students' world, help them see a variety of ways of coping with life's problems, and encourage them to determine for themselves the difference between vice and virtue. This is a wholesome purpose and teachers use good literature to fulfill it.

Censors, said novelist Jerzy Kosinski (1976), "invariably confuse the literary work with the instructional manual, ascribing the same purpose to these two very different kinds of writing: to control the reader's behavior." They see the reader as a robot "destined to imitate the events portrayed in whatever book he or she happens to be reading" (p. 22).

Most people, especially teachers, would probably agree that books can have a powerful influence on people of all ages, but especially on youth. The stories we read or hear as children, and the messages therein, remain with us for a lifetime. Kilpatrick, Wolfe, and Wolfe (1994) wrote, "The power of stories has been vastly underrated in recent decades. The world of books and stories constitutes an enormous but neglected moral resource—a huge treasure house lying largely unused" (p. 21).

Books for young people must be carefully chosen because they do have the potential for molding readers' characters in profoundly moral ways. Stories, said the above authors "inspire a love of goodness. Who can read about King Midas and his golden touch without desiring to always put people before possessions?...Who can read *To Kill a Mockingbird* without wishing to be a little more like Atticus Finch—a little braver, kinder, wiser" (Kilpatrick et al., 1994, pp. 23–24).

In *The Call of Stories* (1989), the psychiatrist and social scientist Robert Coles said he learned from his wife, a high school English teacher, the impact a good novel can have on the tempestuous emotions of teenagers. Literature, he noted, is not meant to be used as replacement for psychotherapy, but "a still growing mind can be exceedingly volatile, can experience wide mood swings, can delight in introspection, can enjoy the pleasures of irony, detachment, satire." As a student told him, "if you 'live' with the book a while...then you'll be part of the story, or it'll be part of you" (p. 63).

Most of Panama City's challenged works received high praise from literary critics, English teachers, librarians, and the general public for many years, not only for the quality of the writing but also for the value of their ethical themes. The novels are definitely not didactic. They do not reflect the RR's desire for absolute purity in all respects, but rather promote within a compelling story a moral stance that could be labeled humanistic, defined in its normal sense (see chap. 2), not the distorted version propagated by the RR.

Writers, teachers, and literary critics point out that stories are based on conflict, and without a clash of values and behaviors there is nothing to relate. Besides, who would want to read a novel where every character personifies goodness as the RR perceives it? Certainly not teenagers—nor their teachers. "Young readers don't need to have heroes of undiluted virtue as long as they are the kind of persons who want to get back on course once they get off it....In a story we meet characters who have something to learn; otherwise we would not be interested in them" (Kilpatrick et al., 1994, pp. 31, 21).

The Bible, which is esteemed not only by the RR but by most people in our country, has many stories of conflict, change, and growth in characters. Evil persons lurk there as well as good, and even Jesus is reported as having times of doubt, anger, and temptation. He learned from them and overcame them, but so do most of the protagonists of the literature condemned by the RR.

Although the religious aspects of a book are important and should be discussed in the classroom setting, students should be encouraged to examine stories from a variety of perspectives, not just one. Good works, explained the Italian poet Italo Calvino (1986) in *The Uses of Literature*, exist on different levels and can be read on several at the same time: "Literature does not recognize Reality as such, but only *levels*" of reality. The more levels there are, the more likely the work will be judged favorably by knowledgeable, intelligent readers and will pass the test of time (p. 120).

Writers often state that they do not set out to write a moral book, but only to tell an interesting story and depict life as they see it. Said Thomas Hardy in 1892 in his preface to the fifth edition of *Tess of the D'Urbervilles*, "A novel is an impression, not an argument" (1965, p. 14). Novelist John Gardner (1983) pointed out that "Good fiction does not deal in codes of conduct—at least not directly; it affirms responsible humanness" (p. 50).

But Gardner also said that "the fiction that lasts tends to be 'moral,' that is, it works with a minimum of cynical manipulation and it tends to reach affirmations favorable rather than opposed to life" (p. 86). Literary critic Northrop Frye (1971), in *The Educated Imagination*, also noted that "literature is not religion, and it doesn't address itself to belief. But if we shut the vision of it completely out of our minds, or insist on its being limited in various ways, something goes dead inside us, perhaps the one thing that it is really important to keep alive" (pp. 80–81). These authors thus accept the idea that morality and religious perceptions are often significant elements in a good book, but stress that they are not the work's *raison d'être*. They should not be the sole criteria for literature selections in public schools, but neither should they be ignored or discounted as unimportant.

Contemporary novelist John Updike, whose works have been attacked for their supposed immorality, wrote, "Surely one of the novel's habitual aims is to articulate morality, to sharpen the reader's sense of vice and virtue" (cited in Booth, 1988, p. 24). Agreeing with this point of view, Robert Coles (1989) said, "Novels and stories are renderings of life; they can not only keep us company, but admonish us, point us in new directions, or give us the courage to stay a given course" (p. 159). Calvino (1986) noted that the morality lies not, however, in the literature itself, which is just a vehicle to convey thought and enhance imagination, but in real-life behavior. Engrossed in a novel, readers continually reflect on their own lives and decisions and those of the created characters, and either reaffirm or alter their personal perceptions of a moral world (p. 36).

Although a writer's goal is to tell a tale, if related well the story will be drenched with ethical dimensions as characters react to situations, make choices, and relate to others. But confronting moral dilemmas encountered by fictional or real characters and evaluating their choices is exactly what the RR objects to. They insist that students be told exactly what to think and how to act according to their RR doctrine. The goal of a literature class in a public school, however, is not to indoctrinate into a particular religious ideology, but to invite discussion, to raise awareness of issues, to debate what in life is wholesome and what is wrong.

ISSUE: DISCUSSION AND DEBATE
OVER BELIEFS AND VALUES

THE RELIGIOUS RIGHT'S CLAIM: Discussion and debate is the religious ideology of secular humanism, whose sole purpose is to denigrate and eliminate Christian beliefs from schools and society.

RR advocates maintain that schools have no right to include on their reading lists and in their libraries books that offend the beliefs of religious people. Children, they believe, do not possess strong enough values and are easily influenced by deviancy. They need to be protected from immoral books, not required or encouraged to read them. RR proponents are dedicated to making sure that their values prevail in public school classrooms, despite what other parents may want, because they are sincerely convinced that they have a mandate to save all of God's children. Said Jerry Falwell (1992):

> If you see a child in the path of an onrushing car and do nothing to prevent the accident, you share the blame for the child's injury. By the same measure, if you see children—whether they are your own or another's—in danger of moral and social disaster through destructive anti-family teaching, you have a responsibility to react quickly and with resolve.
>
> Whether you have school-age children or not, they are your children because they are the community's children. They are your responsibility because God expects you to love and have compassion on your fellow man....You cannot escape your responsibility to the community, and you cannot run from your responsibility to God. (pp. 217–218)

RR advocates say that students need to be taught God-given absolutes and the consequences for those who disobey or disregard them. To discuss and debate moral values as though they are relative and situational is to endanger the lives and souls of America's children.

COUNTERARGUMENT: The freedom to read, discuss, and debate is essential to the preservation of democracy. Students who over time form their own beliefs and values also develop the strength to withstand the negative forces in society.

The great fear of RR parents is that their children will be changed by reading books in school that do not reflect their restricted religious views. The truth is, they are probably right. If books are well chosen and students are actively involved in thinking, discussing, and writing about what they read, chances are they will be affected, but probably for the better.

Katherine Paterson (1981), a winner of the Newberry Award for excellence in writing for children, stated in her nonfiction work, *Gates of Excellence,* that "a great novel is a kind of conversion experience. We come away from it changed" (p. 59). Confronting one's attitudes and beliefs about the world and its inhabitants is an outgrowth of immersing oneself in good literature. The conversion is toward greater understanding of human nature, more tolerance for ambiguity, and an acceptance of others in all their diversity—changes that are consistent with the educational philosophy promoted by public schools.

Calvino (1986) stressed that inherent in literature is the possibility of "questioning the established scale of values and code of meanings" (p. 82). This questioning of what they may have earnestly taught their children is what frightens right-wing parents and leads to charges that schools are undermining parental authority. Believing that young people are easily led astray by those working for the devil (anyone not born again), they want complete control over their offsprings' minds until they reach adulthood. Desiring sincerely to protect their children by giving them the security of a boxed-in world, they cannot risk letting them read or discuss anything that suggests there are different ideas, values, or ways of living that others consider acceptable, even honorable. They dare not let go and give their children room to grow, to think for themselves, to test their own values and beliefs against those of others.

The RR critics of literature thus have legitimate worries. They are correct that one can never be sure what young people will glean from a book. In the first place, children and adolescents do not think like adults and will not view the content of a book in the same way. But even among adults, because of their varied backgrounds, maturity levels, education, and perceptions about life, books will communicate different things to different people and spark emotions not intended by the author or experienced by other readers. And each time a book is read again by the same person, it may evoke new reactions and elicit new conceptions. Calvino (1986) said that each rereading of classic literature "is as much a voyage of discovery as the first reading....The classics help us understand who we are and where we stand" (pp. 127, 133).

One of the main reasons for reading a good book, in fact, is that it takes on a life of its own and leads readers imaginatively into areas and experiences to which they may never have, or want to have, direct access, but that broadens their horizons, strengthens their sensibilities, and enriches their minds. In contrast to RR critics, writers of quality literature say that to value freedom of thought and inquiry is to believe that most humans, including children, are disposed toward good and will use knowledge in constructive ways, especially if encouraged by teachers and other role models. Students will admire the good deeds they read about in books selected for classroom reading, for that will reinforce their values, but are not likely to copy the sinful actions of historical figures or story characters—unless, of course, one views fighting poverty, organizing oppressed workers, or questioning the bombing of undefended cities as sinful.

Novelist Kosinski (1976) pointed out that no matter how engaged readers are in a story, they are still aware of being outside the depicted events and will judge the characters and situations by their own moral code (p. 22). In their sincere wish to protect children from life's harsh realities, RR parents strive to keep away all knowledge and ideas that might cause youngsters to challenge their parents or other authorities or to realize that values and perceptions differ from person to person and culture to culture. Isolated from the rest of the world, they believe, these children will grow up to be strong adults who can withstand outside influences and the inevitable assaults on the values handed them by family and church.

Many writers and teachers have far more faith in young people's common sense, understanding, and desire for goodness. They also believe that children can be harmed by growing up in a cotton-lined world and need to vicariously experience other values, behaviors, and cultures while still in an environment of safety and guidance. Said Nat Hentoff, whose novel about censorship in a public high school, *The Day They Came to Arrest the Book*, has itself been censored:

> Kids who've gone through their secondary school life without ever hearing more than one point of view can become intellectually crippled. They can lose their potential for original and independent thought. They can lose their ability to engage in free inquiry....These parents think that by protecting their children they are making their children more resistant, but actually they are making their children more vulnerable. (cited in West, 1988, p. 64)

According to an editorial in *The American School Board Journal* (*The debate*, 1973), "Good books...tell us how things are. If students are forced to read books that romanticize life and shrink from its less than lovely aspects, then these students may leave school with a distorted—perhaps unhealthy—view of the world as it exists" (p. 39). Noted Daniel Maguire (personal communication, December 1996), "If you raise your children like hothouse plants, they will die in the first storm after they get into the real world."

Kosinski (1976) pointed out that school and books are not the only influencing elements in children's lives, or perhaps even the major ones. The mass media, the reports of violence in the daily news, and the commercialism that exploits sex reach the students no matter how much parents and teachers try to sanitize and isolate the classroom or home. Thus a vital function of education and reading is the following:

> to help students cope with life by exploring with them the realities and ambiguities expressed in recognized literary works. The school offers one of the few structured forums for analyzing such situations—an opportunity to critically evaluate the human condition within the guidelines of literary value and human interchange. (p. 24)

Reading novels and stories, said Robert Coles (1989), is one of the best ways for young people to examine possibilities and problems, to see how they would like to live their own lives. After reading and discussing the themes, characters, and moral aspects of well-chosen books, students "remind themselves of life's contingencies" and "take matters of choice and commitment more seriously than they might otherwise have done" (p. 90).

Thus, quality books do destroy the idyllic picture of a secure, simplistic world that RR advocates want for themselves and their children—and everyone else's children. These works confront readers with the forces of evil and injustice, with social and personal immorality, but also with the forces of good, of love, of generosity, of mercy. They question some values, traditions, and political and religious beliefs, but exhibit others that reinforce democratic, humanistic, more liberal religious values and moral codes. That, say RR proponents, is exactly why they should be banned from schools. That is why many educators and writers, including myself, believe students should be encouraged, perhaps even required, to read them.

4

The Debate Over Biblical Interpretation

Exploring moral and religious issues is not the only or major reason for using selected literature in the classroom, but it is certainly a legitimate and important one. The problem in public schools, however, is determining how morality should be defined, on what basis, and who should decide. The RR claims that the Bible is the only foundation for making moral decisions, whether one is Christian, nonreligious, or a follower of another faith. They vehemently attack literature books on the grounds that they are antibiblical. Passages are taken out of context from both the selected works and the Bible to support their contentions that the works in question are immoral, un-Christian, or irreligious by biblical standards.

English teachers and others, however, have the same right to read the Bible and choose scriptural passages, in or out of context, in defense of challenged works. Even if one reads the Bible literally without scholarly research, alternative views are easily found that can give a quite different perspective on what constitutes biblical morality.

Humanists, whether religious or secular, do not dispute the assertion that the Bible is an appropriate guide for moral behavior. It contains words of great wisdom that are applicable to our lives today. One does not have to be religious to appreciate the moral elements of the Old Testament prophets or the teachings of Jesus. Many passages speak directly to the heart, showing ways to build a better world and offering solace in times of stress. Even agnostics and atheists accept many biblical teachings as a sensible way to live one's life and create harmony in the world.

While he was president of the United States, Thomas Jefferson, a humanist who favored Unitarianism and was attacked for his anti-Christian beliefs, put together all the elements of the New Testament he thought worthy, stating that "of all the systems of morality antient [sic] or modern which have come under my observation, none appear to me so pure as that of Jesus" (cited in Adams, 1983, p. 350). The conflict, thus, lies not in the Bible itself or its acceptance as a moral guide, but in its interpretation.

ISSUE: HOW SHOULD THE BIBLE BE READ?

THE RELIGIOUS RIGHT'S CLAIM: The Bible, read literally, should be the basis for selecting all books in public schools. Any other comes from the Satan-inspired humanism.

In *What Are They Teaching Our Children?* Gabler and Gabler (1985) expressed clearly the polarized thinking of ultraconservatives who oppose public schools:

> Two religions are in mortal combat for the souls and futures of our children and nation. One reverences God and the moral values of the Judeo-Christian Bible. The other rejects God and the Judeo-Christian basis of the American family....The basic issue is simple: which principles will shape the minds of our children? Those which uphold family, morality, freedom, individuality, and free enterprise; or those which advocate atheism, evolution, secularism, and a collectivism in which an elite governs and regulates religion, parenthood, education, property, and the lifestyles of all members of society? (pp. 31–32, 160).

In other words, all teachers, whatever their religion, should base every curricular decision on the Bible, and all students, no matter what their family's religious beliefs, should be taught using only the biblical principles as understood by the RR extremists.

COUNTERARGUMENT: The Bible should not be the basis for the public school curriculum, but it is an important part of Western culture and is thus appropriate to include in academic studies, such as literature classes, along with other Scriptures.

As evidenced by the Gabler quote, a primary characteristic of RR thinking is polarity. Only two sides exist to all things; they are exact opposites and often at war. Said Martin Marty (1987), "Theirs is an almost Manichean world of black/white, God/Satan, Christ/Antichrist, Christian/'secular humanist.' On these terms it is easy to invent and expose 'conspiracies' of the forces against good—good America, good fundamentalists" (p. 300). Most Americans, including probably most educators, see a multisided world in many shades of gray.

A 1992 survey taken by the Gallup Poll showed that Americans' belief in the literal truth of the Bible declined from 65% in 1963, to 38% in 1978, to 32% in 1992. Although almost 50% said they believed the Bible to be the "inspired word of God," that did not mean to them that it was to be taken literally, true in all respects. Furthermore, 69% stated that "situational ethics" was an appropriate means for deciding right and wrong, with 63% rejecting absolutes as a guide to behavior (*Most Americans*, 1992).

The concept of *situation ethics* is viewed differently by different people, but generally means that the particular circumstances must be considered before deciding which behavior would be ethical. For example, lying is usually wrong, but was it so when Huckleberry Finn told bounty hunters that Nigger Jim was White and implied there was smallpox on the raft so they would go away without checking? Stealing is normally bad, but can we blame Jean Valjean in *Les Miserables* for swiping a loaf of bread to feed a starving child? The RR's contention that most people in our society believe moral absolutes should be the guide in all situations is clearly false.

Wrote John Gardner (1983) in *On Becoming a Novelist*:

> Only very odd people don't realize that truth-telling is always a relative value. If you're living in Germany during World War II and a Jew is hiding in your basement, you do nothing wrong in the sight of God by telling the Nazi at your door you're the only one home. Personal integrity (not telling lies) is so obviously bendable in the name of a higher integrity. (p. 51)

Using the Bible as the criterion for materials in public schools would violate the First Amendment. However, the Bible is part of America's cultural heritage and, as we saw in *Abington v. Schempp* (1963; see chapter 1), the Supreme Court has not only condoned but encouraged its use in a scholarly manner in such classes as literature and history, or studies in world cultures and comparative religions. Unless teachers use the same basis as the critics, they cannot effectively demonstrate that selected works have high religious and moral as well as literary worth.

One can also defend books the RR calls immoral with other sources—the Constitution; various philosophies that stress the importance of altruism, simplicity, and right living; the writings of the Founding Fathers; prominent role models who have striven to bring about justice and peace. But because the Bible is what is most frequently used by the RR to attack public schools and literature books, it should also be used to defend them. As Daniel Maguire pointed out in *The Moral Revolution* (1986), the overall themes of the Bible are love, justice, and compassion, especially toward the poor and oppressed (pp. 27–34). As we shall see in Part II, these are the same themes found in literature commonly selected for English classrooms (and attacked by the RR).

From the Bible's rich source, novelists often glean ideas for contemporary conflicts, imaginary characters, and moral dilemmas, as well as phrases and book titles. Without at least a cursory acquaintance with biblical stories and language, teachers and students will miss much of the underlying religiosity, as well as the actual references to themes, persons, statements, and events.

ISSUE: WHO WROTE THE BIBLE
AND HOW SHOULD IT BE USED?

THE RELIGIOUS RIGHT'S CLAIM: The Bible is literally true in all respects. It should not be interpreted, but believed and followed. It is the source of all morality.

Jerry Falwell (1980) said that the Bible "is the inerrant Word of the living God. The Bible is absolutely infallible, without error in all matters pertaining to faith and practice, as well as in areas such as geography, science, history, etc." (p. 63). It is "God's road map of life....It should be the blueprint for your life (1982, pp. 125–126)....There is no mixture of error to be found within its pages" (p. 129).

Tim LaHaye (1992) claimed that fundamentalists, who believe in an "inspired, inerrant, and authoritative Bible" that "offers practical answers for today's problems," are winning the battle for the Bible against those who would take it figuratively or as an allegory. "Lost souls rarely seek out liberal churches that play fast and loose with the Bible" (p. 17).

RR followers believe that if anything in the Bible can be shown to be false, then the whole book must be false, or else it could not be the inspired Word of God. And if the Bible is a fabrication, then the biblical assurance of personal salvation must also be a fraud. Thus, they are dedicated to carrying out what they perceive to be God's will with regard to saving America's morals, standard of living, and children because their eternal future is at stake.

COUNTERARGUMENT: The Bible is an anthology of works, a complex document that is based on the ethics of early times. It contains myths, allegories, poetry, and metaphors, and can be interpreted in many different ways without destroying its beauty and wisdom, or its ability to inspire.

Prominent biblical scholars have provided much evidence that the Bible is not one book, but many, spanning a long period of time, and reflecting the viewpoints of numerous authors in their quest to understand themselves, their fellow beings, their world, and life beyond death.

Despite their contention that every word in the Bible is true, the literalists select only those passages from the Old and New Testaments that support their views, much as Thomas Jefferson did in his extracts from the Gospels. The difference, of course, is that Jefferson made his cuttings consciously and deliberately, under no pretext that this was representative of the rest of the Bible. What he did not approve was left, as Martin Marty (1987) put it, "on the White House study floor" (p. 68), with no fear that a vengeful God would burn down the house, destroy the nation, or consign him to an eternal hell.

A forceful challenge to the RR's claim to biblical inerrancy can be found in Anglican Bishop John Spong's book, *Rescuing the Bible from the Fundamentalists* (1991). The Bible, he said, is "not a literal road map to reality but a historic narrative of the journey our religious forebears made in the eternal human quest to understand life, the world, themselves, and God" (p. 33). The Bible is revered by people of many faiths in our time, because "it touches universal, timeless themes (p. 75)....To literalize the biblical narrative...is to distort and ultimately destroy its truth" (pp. 225–226).

The Bible literalists have a difficult task. They must explain away many conflicting stories and statements, the factual information disproved by modern scientific and historical research, and an abundance of atrocities, much of it reportedly done by God himself. They must also reject a century of scholarship on both the Bible and the social world of early Jewish and Christian communities. According to Wayne Meeks (1986), professor of biblical studies, Yale University:

> Compilation of the moral teachings of the first Christians not only oversimplifies the meaning of those teachings by abstracting them from the social reality within which they functioned, it also encourages Christians today to use the Bible in a way that is often pernicious....[The early Christians] did not have all the answers, and faithfulness is not the same thing as trying to imitate the answers they did have....We must live in our own world, which is irreversibly different from that of the first Christians. (pp. 17, 162).

RR believers particularly abhor the archeology, historical studies, and literary analysis that show the Bible to be an anthology of works, first told orally and then written down by a number of people over a long period of time. The stories, psalms, sayings, and other aspects reflect the ancient authors' understanding of the world, God, human beings, suffering, and purpose of life. They are not, say Bible scholars, to be viewed as literal accounts of history, geography, and science.

Burton L. Mack (1995), professor of New Testament at the School of Theology at Claremont, explained in *Who Wrote the New Testament?* that the Protestant, Catholic, and Hebrew Bibles differ from each other in significant ways. The New Testament is a "small selection of texts from a large body of literature produced by various communities during the first one hundred years" after the death of Jesus. Most of the writings were not written by those whose names are attached to them, but rather, "many minds, voices, and hands were in on the drafting of written materials. No one thought to take credit for writing down community property," and "the later attribution of anonymous literature to known figures of the past...was a standard practice during the Greco-Roman period" (pp. 6–7).

In *The Cultural Subversion of the Biblical Faith* (1977), James D. Smart, professor of biblical interpretation at Union Theological Seminary, wrote:

The Scriptures are a highly complex library of ancient writings that come to us from a succession of ages far distant and different from our own, a million words in sixty-six books of widely different character: prophetic sermons, histories quite unlike any modern histories, folktales, a hymnbook, apostolic letters, gospels—writings produced at various times and in various circumstances over a period of a thousand years in the life of a tiny nation called Israel on the eastern shore of the Mediterranean. (pp. 52–53)

He added that each biblical statement must first be understood within the total context of the particular author's writings, and then in the larger context of the whole Bible. Thus, a literal reading of isolated texts leads not only to misunderstanding, but is nonsensical in light of the thousand years of history that went into the creation of the 66 books (p. 54).

Many passages in the Bible advocate a high level of personal and societal morality that is both inspirational and difficult to attain. Other passages record societal norms that Western culture has humanely abandoned. Using the Bible as an absolute guide for moral behavior in our present-day multicultural democracy is problematic as well as pernicious. The Bible reflects many beliefs about the world that prevailed in a primitive, prescientific age that are either impossible or impractical to use as a guide for modern-day life.

Wrote church historian R. Joseph Hoffmann (1988) at La Trobe University, Melbourne, Australia, in his preface to *Biblical and Secular Ethics: The Conflict*, "As the race between technology and human values poses unprecedented questions concerning the criteria of 'moral' action, the Bible cannot help but show its roots in the tribal and customary laws of the ancient Near East" (p. 7). He noted further:

A book that teaches the inferiority of women, the permissibility of slavery, the ostracism of non-Jews (and later, non-Christians), the stoning of disobedient sons, the necessity of blood-feud and vengeance, and a dozen other unsavory attitudes and rules, scarcely qualifies as an instrument of intellectual and social liberation. (pp. 7–8)

In the first chapter of *The Moral Core of Judaism and Christianity* (1993), Daniel Maguire gave not only biblical examples but also contemporary ones of slaughter and cruelty done in the name of the Lord. "Ancient fathers," he wrote, "slew their children at the altar in the cause of military success and security." Today "our military high priests have long seemed ready to sacrifice the planet itself" (p. 10). We spend huge amounts of money and use our technical genius:

to make unneeded weapons while poverty abounds, national debts mount, and economies erode, accelerating the probability of nuclear holocaust as this power for human extinction proliferates in a desperate and overpopulating world....The more we do of what we are doing, the less secure we are. Such ritualized waste fits better in the categories of religious fanaticism. (p. 11)

Yet, he asserted, the original ideals of Christianity and Judaism and other religions as well remain a source of moral power that "could have a major, transforming impact on our modernity" (p. 3).

In *Who Needs God* (1989), Rabbi Harold Kushner wrote that in addition to the Bible, "we have tradition, thousands of years of insight, experience, trial-and-error carried out by people of profound spiritual sensitivity and caring." Though he personally believes that the Bible contains the best explanation of God's will on moral issues, "it was God's first word on the subject, not His last. The last word has not been heard yet" (p. 85).

Religious people of many faiths disagree on what is meant by *biblical principles*. In our democracy anyone can sing the song, *The Bible Tells Me So*. To illustrate the differences in interpretation between right-wing fundamentalists and those who read the Bible nonliterally, television commentator Bill Moyers, who grew up in the Southern Baptist tradition, pointed out that war images are frequently used by the RR to explain their religious values. For instance, Pat Buchanan has repeatedly asserted that the RR is engaged in a *holy war* or a *cultural war* with liberals, humanists, feminists, homosexuals, and all the other groups he condemns.

Ralph Reed said that "only Christian believers...in the thick of battle" (cited in Moyers, 1995, p. 16) can take back this country and its schools and make them moral. Although he has tried to distance himself in recent years from his earlier colorful words,[1] Reed spoke proudly in 1991 of using *stealth tactics* and *guerrilla warfare* to win school board and other elections, "I want to be invisible. I paint my face and travel at night. You don't know it's over until you're in a body bag. You don't know until election night" (cited in Boston, 1996b, p. 91).

This militant rhetoric, said Moyers, is a throwback to the Crusades of the Middle Ages, where "the teacher Jesus who had talked of loving one's neighbor and forgiving one's enemy, who had looked with compassion on the wounded and sick...who had gathered to him the outcast and stranger, the despised and forsaken...was now yoked to the cause of flashing shield and slashing sword, politics and conquest" (1995, p. 16).

The Bible, in other words, can be used by those who advocate warlike means to attack their religious and cultural enemies as well as by those who promote harmony and peace. It can also be used to both accuse and defend literature books used in classrooms. The Bible does not belong to any one group. We all have the right to read and interpret it for ourselves. That was the point of the Protestant Reformation, which resulted in the Puritan tradition so revered by the RR.

---

[1]See chapter 6 in R. Reed, *Active Faith* (1996).

I agree with biblical scholars that segments need to be studied in their context to ascertain their true meaning and significance. However, in Part II, I use the RR approach and choose biblical passages in defense of literature without regard to what comes before or after, or the historical setting. My reason is to illustrate that even when read literally—or especially when read literally—one will find many conflicting statements in the Bible. Quite likely for every passage I use to defend the moral content of selected literature, an RR opponent could quote another that says the opposite—which is exactly my point. Contradictions are a problem only for the literalists, not for those who view the Bible as a collection of works to be read on many levels and interpreted in ways meaningful to those who read it, and who recognize both its connection to ancient mores and its relevance to the modern world.

Thus, even if educators and RR followers agree that the Bible is a good source for moral guidance, a legitimate means of determining the ethical quality of a literary work, and a constitutionally approved element of academic discussions, the selection and interpretation of biblical evidence and its application to present-day society remains perhaps an uncompromisable problem.

5

The Debate Over Morality in Literature

As we have seen, RR leaders have for decades assailed public schools and accused teachers of undermining parental values, denigrating the Christian religion, and promoting immorality. A major source of conflict in this battle over education and moral values is the literature selected for classroom reading or school libraries.

Prominent among the book protestors are Gabler and Gabler (1985), who charged that the works chosen for reading in most public schools "contribute to rebellion, lack of respect for authority, sadism, violence, and disillusionment" (p. 94). Teachers use these books, they maintain, to manipulate students' attitudes and beliefs rather than enrich their lives "through reading fine classics" (p. 95). Because literary critics, English teachers, and non-RR parents believe that many of the works found on censorship lists are fine classics, book selection sometimes elicits a confrontation over evaluation and judgment.

This chapter examines several of the most common charges leveled against literature in general, along with some possible responses. The accusations and reasons are given so that educators can know what they are likely to hear when confronted with RR objectors. They are summaries of statements I have gathered over the years from books, articles, speeches, interviews, students, and audience participators.

The counterarguments are from my own religious background and educational philosophy, supported by statements gleaned mostly from serendipitous reading. They in no way exhaust the possibilities for refuting the charges made against books, but are offered here as a starting point, food for thought, and encouragement to resist the intimidation tactics of the accusers and to develop moral as well as literary rationales for quality works.

In Part II we look more specifically at six books that have long been on censorship lists, some of the reasons for the attacks, and some ways to defend and promote their moral value in both biblical and humanistic terms. Although I wrote those chapters before I read Harold Kushner's book *When All You've Ever Wanted Isn't Enough* (1986), I found in one of his statements the essence of what I believe about life and why good stories about the experiences of others, fictional or real, help readers ask questions, find solutions, try out various paths, and live their lives more fully: "Life," he said, "is not a problem to be solved once; it is a continuing challenge to be lived day by day. Our quest is not to find the Answer but to find ways of making each individual day a human experience" (p. 143).

Good literature helps us in this quest; so can the Bible, that wonderful collection of stories, poems, sayings, and psalms. Both contain many kinds of experiences that readers can relate to, as well as ethical conflicts and moral challenges. The purpose of reading the Bible, other Scriptures, and other literature, I believe, is not to discover the one true way to think and behave, but to enlarge our world, deepen our sensibilities, affirm the goodness of life, and learn what it means to be human.

ISSUE: BAD LANGUAGE

THE RELIGIOUS RIGHT'S CLAIM: Profane, blasphemous, vulgar language and sexual references and connotations are immoral, undermine religious values taught at home, and have no place in novels given to adolescents and younger children.

Because of their absolutist, polarized stance, RR proponents believe that a book is either totally good or totally bad, and one automatic determination of badness is the inclusion of any words considered blasphemous, vulgar, or related to sexual relations no matter what the circumstance.

RR followers maintain that students should not be exposed to any books that contain *filth*. There is no need to confront young readers with such words and images when they are immature and still forming their values. Teachers and parents need to keep children's minds clean and teach them the language of civility, not degradation, blasphemy, and obscenities.

Writing, speaking, or even looking at printed language that is blasphemous, sex related, or scatological, no matter how devoid of religious connotations or what the intent or situation, is regarded by the RR as a sin. They believe that just seeing such words will harm children, and Christians will be punished by their God if they do not remove these books from schools, libraries, and society.

Historian Ralph Barton Perry (1944), in describing the Puritan mindset, explained that sin is seen as "contagious." Just being in close proximity to evil conditions can be dangerous. Thus, RR conservatives are convinced that they have a command from God to clean up the environment to protect themselves and others, especially children. Said Perry, "Ideas and sentiments, like disease, are spread by contact." It is thus necessary to get rid of "bad" beliefs as well as "bad" believers, which makes religion a public rather than a private matter (p. 329); hence, the attempt of today's Christian Coalition to take over all the nation's schools, elected offices, and the Republican party.

COUNTERARGUMENT: Words are neutral. Their power to offend lies in the reader's religious and social background, which varies from culture to culture and age to age.

RR followers have an overwhelming belief in the power of words and greatly fear the influence of books on immature minds (or even adult ones). Nat Hentoff, whose own works have elicited the censors' wrath, said, "They truly feel that words have the power to transform a child, to turn a child inside out. At the same time, they do not have as much confidence in the child's ability to make sound decisions" (cited in West, 1988, p. 63).

To other minds, however, *dirty words* are only bad because someone says they are. They have no power unto themselves. Said linguist Hugh Rawson in *Wicked Words* (1989), "The power of a word as well as its meaning depends greatly on the setting in which it is used....The ultimate absurdity is reached when fearful people search for 'bad' meanings where none exist" (p. 4).

In fact, the more such words are said or read, the less impact they have. For teenagers, these words are often a way to feel grownup—and a lot less harmful than other means they could choose. A major task of adolescence is to cut the ties of dependency from parents and other adults and assert one's individuality. Using language not approved by adults is one way to do that; it gives young people a sense of control over their lives by rebelling against external authority and setting their own standards.

That does not mean teachers or parents should encourage uncivil language in youth or ignore it completely, but understand its attraction and refuse to let it anger or alarm. Objectionable words should not be used in polite society or deliberately said to offend someone's religious beliefs or moral sensibilities, but the offense is in the ear of the hearer and not in the words themselves. In fact, the repeated use of obscenities shows a lack of original thought and facility with words that is much more corrupting to the English language than to anyone's morals.

Although words used by characters in commonly assigned books may indeed be vulgar, they are seldom blasphemous, which is "the act of vilifying or ridiculing the divine Being, the Bible, the church, or the Christian religion" (Montague, 1967, p. 101). Those who say *Goddamit* are not reviling God. If anything, they are asking God to damn a particularly exasperating situation. In reality, the speaker is probably not thinking in religious terms at all. According to Ashley Montague in *The Anatomy of Swearing* (1967), such expressions as *God damn you, blast you,* and *go to hell* have their origins in curses of the medieval church (p. 64). Blasphemy was superseded by *heresy*, which means "false doctrine," and eventually the two were united in New World Protestantism (Levy, 1981, pp. 113, 121).

The purpose of using profanity, said Montague (1967), is neither to vilify nor ridicule anything connected to religion, but to relieve tension. No irreverence is intended. Rather its function, which is common to human beings in all cultures, is to act as an effective substitute for aggressive feelings and frustrations caused by such things as shocks, disappointments, surprises, and humiliations (pp. 69, 73).

Curiously, the wrathful God worshipped by the RR is evidently not bothered if letters are substituted or synonyms used. Thus *dadgum, goldarn, Good Lord, My Word,* and *Heavens* are acceptable even to many fundamentalists, but not *Goddam, Good God,* or *hell.* Or one can substitute *golly* or *gosh* for *God, heck* or *blazes* for *hell,* or *Gee, Gee-whizz,* or *Jeeze* for *Jesus* without fear of either societal or supernatural condemnation (McDonald, 1988, pp. 61, 63, 64; Rawson, 1989, p. 190). If God is angry over the use of real words, should He not be even more wrathful over the attempt to slip something by Him by changing letters?

Rawson (1989) noted that the reaction to bad words is directly related to a person's religious background:

> Where the most taboo words in Roman Catholic countries tend to be the blasphemous ones—oaths in the name of the Father, Son, or Virgin Mary—the truly offensive terms for Protestants are those that refer to intimate parts of the body and its functions...Protestants generally are more terrified of their bodies than their Lord. (pp. 6–7).

Obscenity, he pointed out, is "essentially a function of social class. It always involves words that are, by definition, vulgar," which stems from the Latin *vulgaris,* meaning "common people" (p. 8). Thus, those who do not want to be considered common or lower class refrain from using such words, at least socially. This, however, is historically a fairly recent attitude. "Until the early 1700s" said Rawson, "even refined people casually used what later came to be regarded as low words" (p. 9). Middle-class morality came into the American colonies and England toward the end of the 1700s when Victorianism was in full bloom. In the early 1800s, efforts to eliminate vulgarisms were vigorously pursued by expurgators such as Thomas Bowdler, who wished to remove all words from previously published literature that would offend the women and children of his own time.[1]

Furthermore, the *vulgar* words objected to in these books were not deemed obscene in biblical times, for the concept did not even exist. In fact, as Rawson (1989) pointed out, some of the words are used in the Bible. The King James translation of 1611, for instance, includes *dung, piss,* and *whore*

---

[1]Thomas Bowdler's efforts brought into English usage the term *bowdlerize,* meaning to expurgate prudishly.

(Rawson, p. 9). The concept of *obscenity* as a moral offense did not come into being until the 17th century (p. 9). The words were accepted by society as immoral when Puritan beliefs ruled New England because that is what the religious leaders taught. The Old World church, however, had only punished for blasphemy or heresy, not vulgarity.

The *worst word in the English language* is simply a coarse term for intercourse, and is seldom actually used in that sense. More often, in today's slang, it is an adjective showing disgust, such as a *fuckin' car* that won't start. The other *dirtiest word* refers to the product of a necessary biological function, but again is more often used as an expletive expressing frustration. Many who object to the word *shit* freely substitute the word *shoot* with no thought of being vulgar or obscene.

Language, which is easy to document without even reading a work, often masks other objections and goals. "Language is the censor's foot in the door," said children's story writer Harry Mazar:

> The censors have certain ideas about what children should read. They want exemplary books that teach proper behavior. They want books with happy endings and neat little moral homilies. They want models of goodness, children who don't use 'bad' words or talk up to their elders, or God forbid, even think about sex. They want children fenced out of the real world.....They want...books to present a safe, predictable, sugarcoated world, a world that never was and never will be. (cited in West, 1988, pp. 55–56)

Because they believe the books used in public schools are sinful and sin is contagious, the RR cannot protect their own children from the influence of books that are on shelves or read by other students. There is no inoculation that will give them immunity from wrong ideas and anti-Christian values. The only solution, the only way to keep young people from being exposed to what they find objectionable, they believe, is to force the removal of offensive books from schools and libraries. However, this is not censorship, they claim, but the constitutional exercising of their parental rights in overseeing the upbringing of their children.

ISSUE: FAMILY VALUES AND FEMINISM

THE RELIGIOUS RIGHT'S CLAIM: The primary purpose of humanistic teachers assigning offensive books is to attack the traditional American family and promote the radical, sinful feminist agenda.

The only biblically approved way of living for most humans, according to the RR, is the *traditional family*, which consists of a heterosexual, monogamous, lifelong marriage between a man and woman who have several biological or adopted children. The husband is the head of the family and the wife his dependent, stay-at-home helpmate. All deviations from this—divorce, premarital or extramarital sex, unwed mothers, homosexuality, unmarrieds living together, and single-parent adoptions—are sinful. Working mothers were formerly included in this list, but given several decades of economic difficulties, the number of divorces and single mothers, and the desirability of two incomes, RR leaders have backed off somewhat from this issue while still maintaining that stay-at-home wives and mothers are what God has in mind.

Falwell (1980) maintained that the roles of the genders are "designated by God. God's plan is for men to be manly and spiritual in all areas of leadership...women are to be feminine and manifest the 'ornament of a meek and quiet spirit'....In the Christian home the woman is to be submissive" (p. 183). Those who decline to accept these roles live in "disobedience to God's laws" (p. 150).

The worst enemies are feminists, who have declared "open war on the family" (Falwell, 1992, p. 205). The RR finds ample evidence in the Bible to support their view. Women who strive for equal educational and career opportunities, equal pay, and equality in the home, for instance, flout the God-created male authority. The Bible says that God has called the father to be the head of the family (Eph. 5:23).[2] A man's task is to exercise authority, make decisions, and provide economic wealth and protection. Wives are to submit to his wisdom and cheerfully carry out his wishes (Eph. 5:22; Col. 3:18). Other biblical passages state:

"I suffer not a woman . . . to usurp authority over the man, but to be in silence." I Tim. 2:12

"For Adam was first formed, then Eve." I Tim. 2:13

"The head of every man is Christ; and the head of the woman is the man." I Cor. 11:3

"Thy desire shall be to thy husband, and he shall rule over thee." Gen. 3:16

Southern Baptist minister Rick Scarborough denounced the "wicked secular humanist lie of feminism" and charged that because America has forgotten God, women have fallen into "insubordination," which he called the "ultimate perversion of womanhood" (cited in Conn, 1996b, p. 12). Tim LaHaye (1982) wrote that "the refusal to face the differences between men and women borders on intellectual insanity...women, not men, instinctively yearn to nurture, love, and care for the young....The feminist movement is in part a fight against God and nature" and "is the ultimate in selfishness" (p. 145).

---

[2]Biblical references are from *The Holy Bible*, King James version (1995). Grand Rapids, MI: Zondervan.

Pat Robertson stated in a fund-raising letter to his Christian Coalition constituents, "The feminist agenda is not about equal rights for women. It is about a socialist, anti-family political movement that encourages women to leave their husbands, kill their children, practice witchcraft, destroy capitalism and become lesbians" (cited in Boston, 1996b, p. 164). Phyllis Schlafly (1984) objected to books and teachers who "blur traditional concepts of gender identity and force the child to accept the radical notion of a gender-free society in which there are no differences in attitudes and occupations between men and women" (p. 437). Textbooks that show women in jobs requiring hard physical labor and men performing domestic household duties are objectionable because of the unbiblical role reversals. Schlafly is also bothered by stories in which children help their parents solve problems, which undermines parental authority.

America's traditional family, say those of the RR, is what has made this country great and any modification of that will bring America down. Thus any reading material that shows or discusses other kinds of families, lifestyles, or living arrangements contributes to this destruction.

COUNTERARGUMENT: Public schools and teachers are not attacking the traditional family as defined by the RR, which in fact has a short-lived history. Society as a whole views the family in other terms, and the feminist movement for equality between the sexes is not a threat to true family values.

A 1990 public opinion survey, the MassMutual American Family Values Study, commissioned by the Massachusetts Mutual Life Insurance Company, reported that the most striking finding was that "Americans overwhelmingly cast the family in emotional, rather than legal or structural terms. Nearly three-fourths (74%) of respondents defined family as 'a group who love and care for each other.' Only about one in five (22%) chose 'a group of people related by blood, marriage or adoption'" (Salk, 1990, p. 9).

Furthermore, according to a study presented at the 1996 International Conference on Infant Studies in Providence, Rhode Island, placing an infant in child care is not likely, in itself, to jeopardize the mother–child bond. The study clearly indicated that "nonmaternal child care by itself does not constitute a threat to the security of the infant–mother attachment," although poor quality of child care or excessive amounts may be damaging (Cohen, 1996, p, 7).

Family historian Stephanie Coontz (1996) reported in her research that the RR's conception of the traditional family is a fairly recent and short-spanned phenomenon. Until the 1950s the nuclear family was not the norm. Many households took in boarders, lodgers, or unmarried relatives who were integrated into family life, and mothers frequently contributed to the income with home careers, such as teaching, sewing, and writing, or worked alongside husbands on the farm or in family businesses. Not until the 1920s were a majority of children born to male-breadwinner, female-homemaker families.

During the Depression in the 1930s, divorce rates fell, said Coontz, but desertion and domestic violence rose sharply. Murder rates in the 1930s were as high as in the 1980s and the rates of marriages and births plummeted. World War II started a marriage boom as young men left for the armed services, but by the end of the war the number of divorces was double that in 1941. Thus, what the RR describes as the traditional family was an aberration of a single decade, the 1950s. During this time, the age of marriage and parenthood dropped dramatically, divorce rates bottomed out, and the birthrate "approached that of India" (p. 41).

Stated Coontz, "Taking the 1950s as the traditional norm overstates both the novelty of modern family life and the continuity of tradition. The 1950s was the most atypical decade in the entire history of American marriage and family life" (p. 41). Families in the 1990s, she maintained, are closer to older patterns than those of the 1950s. The median age at first marriage resembles the beginning of the century, the proportion of never-marrieds is lower, the number of women providing financial support and the proportion of children living in stepfamilies are closer to Colonial days than the 1950s. Furthermore, "the time a modern working mother devotes to childcare is higher than in Colonial or Revolutionary days" (p. 42).

Besides being nontraditional, said Coontz, the 1950s nuclear family was not idyllic. Alcoholism, wife- and child-battering, and incest were swept under the rug, as was discrimination against ethnic groups, political dissidents, women, elders, gays, lesbians, religious minorities, and the mentally or physically challenged. Thirty percent of children lived in poverty, a figure as high as the first half of the 1990s. The economic situation improved for many people in the 1950s, but that had nothing to do with family arrangements and everything to do with strong unions, government benefits, the GI education bill, home mortgage deductions, and increased Social Security payments.

But what about the Bible? Can the statements ordering women to submit to their husbands be countered with other biblical passages? Because the Bible, as noted in chapter 4, reflects the times and social mores of ancient times, few statements directly dispute those that posit male power based on the belief in female inferiority. One must look to the broader messages and to the reports in the New Testament concerning Jesus' interaction with women.

Daniel Maguire argued in *The Moral Revolution* (1986) that because marriage should be based on mutual respect and the encouragement of each partner's uniqueness, "feminism is friendly to marriage. The fact that when some women become feminist, their marriages fail, does not indict the woman seeking mutuality, but the man denying it" (p. 81). Marriage, he pointed out, requires also forgiveness, trust, freedom, and of course love, all of which are abundantly advocated in both Testaments. "Jesus," said Maguire, "appears as a revolutionary feminist in his behavior and teaching....All four Gospels show women as prominent in the public life of Jesus" (p. 132). After discussing the many ways women figured in the early church, Maguire admitted that the Christian scriptures "are not free of ambivalent and negative attitudes toward women in the community," because the "culture was fighting back against the egalitarian revolution started by Jesus, and it made inroads" (pp. 132–133).

But even the Apostle Paul, who stated bluntly, "It is a shame for women to speak in the church" and "if they will learn anything, let them ask their husbands at home" (Cor. 14:35), also said more generously, "There is neither Jew nor Greek, there is neither bond nor free, there is neither male nor female: for ye are all one in Christ Jesus" (Gal. 3:28), thus pronouncing a new concept of equality between the sexes.

The letter to Timothy, attributed to Paul but which New Testament scholar Burton Mack (1995) said is "thoroughly un-Pauline" and most likely from another's hand (p. 206), states that women should keep silent, not usurp power over men, nor braid their hair (I Tim. 2:9–12). However, it also says, "Neglect not the gift that is in thee" (I Tim. 4:14). Women were no doubt excluded from this statement, given the author's belief that they were often idlers, tattlers, and busybodies (I Tim. 5:13), but if in Christ Jesus there is neither male nor female, a woman who neglects her talents is as guilty as a man of offending the Creator of life.

Thus, evidence is found in both American history and the Bible that disputes the RR contention regarding the past strength and sacredness of the traditional American family and the sinfulness of the feminist movement for sexual equality.

ISSUE: RELIGION

THE RELIGIOUS RIGHT'S CLAIM: The books used in public schools attack Christian beliefs and teach New Age religion, witchcraft, and Satanism.

Pat Robertson (1991) called "demonic" the "New Age religion," which he declared that teachers promote, comparing it to the "occultism" practiced by the leaders of Nazi Germany in their "ghastly programs for world domination" (pp. 9, 168). Robert Simonds, who has made a career out of lambasting public schools, insists that the goal of teachers is to open children's minds "to seances and witchcraft for physical and psychological euphoria, elation, ecstasy, wellness, relaxation, enhanced mental powers, sensory and physical sensations as well as stress relief"—all of which in his mind are antireligious and antifamily and will destroy children's belief in God (cited in Kaplan, 1994, p. K7).

Simonds claimed that 47% of an assessment program called Outcomes-Based Education, used in some school districts to evaluate students on both cognitive and affective learning, is comprised of "witchcraft, shamanism, black magic, necromancy (talking to the dead), hypnotism, and psychological manipulation of children's minds" (cited in Kaplan, 1994, p. K6). "Satan," he said, "uses the evil in the occult, new-age witchcraft lessons in our classrooms to divert our children's faith away from the true and living God" (Etzioni, 1996, p. 40).

Any literature that includes depictions of witches, the devil, or Halloween are prime targets for the RR censors. Thus the Hawthorne story *Young Goodman Brown* and Arthur Miller's play *The Crucible* about the Salem, Massachusetts, witch-hunts have frequently been challenged.

In the 1987 censorship case, *Mozert v. Hawkins County, Tennessee*, the RR plaintiffs objected to the Holt Rinehart reading series that included, among other classics, excerpts from *The Wizard of Oz*, because of the wizard, the witches, and Dorothy's psychological flight back to Kansas by kicking her heels and believing in her ability to return home. Because RR leaders have objected to the use of rainbows as classroom decorations because of their use on New Age posters and other paraphernalia, the "Somewhere Over the Rainbow" song from the Judy Garland movie may also have played a part in this challenge.

Another elementary school reading series, *Impressions*, which uses world literature, myths, fables, and folk tales, has been vehemently attacked across the nation, partially because it contains poems and stories on Halloween, which the RR claims teach witchcraft and Satanism.[3]

The children's book *Halloween ABC*, by poet Eve Merriam, has also been challenged in classrooms and libraries because it allegedly contains satanic references, cult symbols, and promotes violent and deviant behavior. Beyond any redemption, to some critics, are the recent Albert Schwarz *Scary Stories* series and the *Goosebumps* books by R. L. Stine, which admittedly other parents also object to because of the violent and gross content.

Another element that RR leaders condemn is anything on non-Christian religions. Public school teachers, claimed Falwell (1992), can teach "all kinds of Eastern religions and New Age mysticism 'as literature' without a hint of criticism, but students *on their own*, cannot read from the Bible or talk about Christian values in school" (p. 214). The plaintiffs in the *Mozert* case also attacked the Holt-Rinehart reading series, not because religion was censored from the books, but because facts about religious beliefs and practices other than fundamentalist Christianity were included in the stories.

---

[3]Pat Robertson, who views Halloween as a Satanic plot, wrote, "Do you want your children to dress up like witches? The Druids used to dress up like this when they were doing human sacrifice. . . . [Your children] are acting out Satanic rituals" (cited in Boston, 1996b, p. 171).

The Gablers (1985) maintained that they do not object to teaching facts about other religions, but only to "teaching-as-fact the relativistic premise that all religions are products of human imagination" (p. 39). Their antagonism toward other religious beliefs throughout their book, however, belies this open-mindedness toward teaching about other religions. Despite the occasional disclaimers, in the writings of all of the prominent RR leaders can be seen the demand that only the narrow religious beliefs of the extreme right be included in anything that is related to religion (and *everything* is related). All other viewpoints come from Satan and, for the protection of all children, must be driven out of public schools.

COUNTERARGUMENT: To claim that public schools are hostile to Christianity, teach witchcraft and occultism, and hypnotize students for Satanic purposes is an outrageous charge against all the hard-working, conscientious teachers who have dedicated their lives to educating students in a multicultural, multireligious, democratic society.

RR leaders spend much time and money attacking all nonfundamentalist beliefs, and making bizarre and vicious assertions against public school educators and books. They then loudly scream "Nazism" when their own beliefs are criticized by those they have slandered and bullied. As Martin Marty pointed out, America's longest and strongest tradition is religious pluralism. Although Protestant Christianity dominated public schools until the 1960s, and still does in many regions of the country, it was and is a flagrant violation of the First Amendment's freedom of religion clause.

Modern-day RR proponents are determined to impose their beliefs on all public school students because of their conviction that they alone know God's will and everyone else is wrong, deceived by the devil. According to Ralph Barton Perry (1944), the 17th-century Puritans (like RR believers today) believed that having taken God's side it was natural to assume that God had taken theirs, and that "Satan was on the side of the enemies" (p. 252). The assumption of what is God's side and what is Satan's, of course, is in the mind of the believer.

The RR's claim that all religious beliefs except theirs are currently being taught in public schools, or that schools teach the "religion of secular humanism," is simply not true. As discussed in chapter 2, humanism is a philosophy, not a religion (unless religion is so broadly defined as to include everything), and the tenets of particular faiths are only taught when relevant to academic subject matter. This is not done often in most classes, especially because teachers have been intimidated by the belligerent and unfair charges of the RR.

Where a discussion of religion is appropriate, such as in literature, history, or world culture classes, the teacher's goal is to remain neutral and allow a variety of ideas, informational aspects, and opinions to be put forth for students' consideration. What the RR accusers want, however, is not an objective, neutral discussion of various religions and beliefs, but the teaching of RR dogma and values only. When other belief systems are encountered in books, they insist that students be told that these are un-Christian and false.

Also, as we saw in chapter 1, the RR critics are wrong in saying that children are not allowed to pray and that the Bible has been banned from public schools. Children can pray silently whenever they wish and, although individual teachers or school administrators may mistakenly interpret the Supreme Court's 1963 decision as meaning children cannot read the Bible voluntarily on their own time, there is no court or nationwide mandate against it. The Court's ruling banned only state-sponsored religious rituals in public schools, and the justices encouraged the use of the Bible in academic courses when relevant.

One of the major reasons RR believers frequently attack literature books used in schools is that acclaimed authors do not share the RR's viewpoint regarding God, humans, or the world. In that respect, they have a point that their right-wing fundamentalism is not represented in school. Finding quality literature that reflects RR beliefs would indeed be a challenge for teachers. Students from RR families, however, have the same right as all other students, when appropriate, to express their opinions orally or in writing about the religious elements in books and to compare these elements to their own belief system. In critiquing papers or arguments on religion, teachers must be careful to utilize the same objective standards they use with all other assignments. Just because a composition is about religion does not protect it from professional evaluation, as RR students and parents sometimes argue, claiming that a poorly written paper was given a low mark because of the Christian beliefs expressed.

Besides the fact that writers of literature commonly used in English courses do not share RR beliefs about religion, they do not agree with each other, which is why discussing a book's presentation of religious and moral beliefs in class is such an interesting and engaging endeavor. It raises many intriguing questions—the very ones the RR believers do not want raised for fear their children will examine the religion given them by their parents and find it wanting. For instance, where does the idea of God come from? Why do people disagree so drastically? What is a mature, authentic religion and what hinders a person's spiritual development?

Psychologist M. S. Peck, in his best-seller, *The Road Less Travelled* (1978), wrote:

> Our first (and sadly, often our only) notion of God's nature is a simple extrapolation of our parents' natures, a simple blending of the characters of our mothers and fathers or their substitutes. If we have loving, forgiving parents, we are likely to believe in a loving and forgiving God. And in our adult view the world is likely to seem as nurturing a place as our childhood

was. If our parents were harsh and punitive, we are likely to mature with a concept of a harsh and punitive monster-god. And if they failed to care for us, we will likely envision the universe as similarly uncaring. (pp. 190–191)

Peck continued, "There is no such thing as a good hand-me-down religion. To be vital, to be the best of which we are capable, our religion must be a wholly personal one, forged entirely through the fire of our questioning and doubting in the crucible of our own experience of reality" (p. 194).

Rabbi Harold Kushner (1986) agreed with this viewpoint: "Religion should not be in the position of giving us answers. It should give us courage to find our own way" and should "even encourage us to challenge its own positions critically" (p. 130). "True religion should not say to us, 'Obey! Conform! Reproduce the past!' It should call upon us to grow, to dare, even to choose wrongly at times and learn from our mistakes rather than being repeatedly pulled back from the brink of using our own minds" (p. 132).

Such religion also does not advocate that believers tremble in fear of a wrathful God, or grovel, or blindly obey their interpretation of Scriptures, said Kushner. The "fear of God" does not mean being afraid but having awe and reverence (p. 131). "Where fear makes us want to run away, awe makes us want to draw closer even as we hesitate to get too close....We stand openmouthed in appreciation of something greater than ourselves" (p. 131). Furthermore, "a religion which persists in understanding 'good' to mean 'unquestioningly obedient,' is a religion which would make perpetual children of us all" (p. 128).

Thus sincere, spiritual, intelligent people dedicated to their particular faith can differ quite drastically in their perception of what constitutes authentic religion. Educators should not be intimidated by anyone who claims to speak for God, who calls all other religions *Satan-inspired*, and who demands that their religious beliefs be taught in public schools.

The First Amendment requires state agents such as teachers to be religiously neutral and not promote religious belief over nonbelief, or some religious beliefs over others. However, talking about religious ideas and beliefs, such as those found in works of literature, is an acceptable and worthy academic endeavor. A dilemma arises, however, when a religious group such as the RR claims it is against their religion for their children to read about or discuss any religious ideas except their own. The Constitution protects the freedom to exercise one's religion, as long as that practice does not tread on the rights of others or undermine democratic principles. The Constitution does not protect people from hearing ideas with which they disagree, even if their religion forbids it. Teachers must stand firm against the attempt of the RR, or anyone else, to twist the First Amendment into a weapon that limits the education of other people's children, restricts the books that are available, and censors the ideas therein.

ISSUE: IMAGINATION AND FANTASY

THE RELIGIOUS RIGHT'S CLAIM: Stories that take students into the realm of fantasy are dangerous to students' mental health. Children's imaginations need to be bounded.

RR believers claim that when children are encouraged to use their imaginations in school, they are being led away from biblical truths and the knowledge they need to function well in their future lives. When teachers give fantasy or science fiction stories to students of any age they are fooling around with their minds. Teachers are supposed to teach objective knowledge, not play mind games with children.

In these stories, characters not only travel through space and time, but sometimes engage in mental telepathy, which the RR considers blasphemous. The ability to read people's thoughts belongs to God alone. Attempting to share that power reflects a sinful humanistic desire to take the place of God. Students, the RR claims, need to learn the skills necessary to live on this earth, not imagine impossibilities like time travel and, what is worse, transmogrification. Reading or writing such stories only encourages children to *space out* and escape reality.

Instead of creating or reading about false worlds and fake science, say RR proponents, students should learn factual information that will help them go to college or technical schools, get good jobs or be good homemakers, and contribute to society in responsible ways. They should be taught truth, not lies about unreal worlds. "Truth," said Jesus "shall make you free" (John 8:32). Anything else is a ridiculous waste of time, an insult to students' intelligence, a psychological travesty, and an injustice to the children's future.

COUNTERARGUMENT: Encouraging children to use their imaginations to visualize performing a skill well, to create a story, or to envision a different world is not mind control, hypnotism, or evidence of the occult. It is an important part of education because a highly developed imagination is essential in every discipline, from the arts to science.

Anthony Storr (1988), in his book on the many benefits of solitude, wrote, "Even science depends more upon phantasy than Freud acknowledged. Many scientific hypotheses take origin from flights of the imagination which at first seem wild, but which later stand up to sober scrutiny and detailed proof," such as Newton's theory of gravity, Kekule's ring-structure of organic molecules, and Einstein's theory of relativity (p. 67). A people who "lacked the capacity for phantasy would not only be unable to imagine a better life in material terms, but would also lack religion, music, literature, and painting" (pp. 66-67).

Furthermore, banning products that come from religious belief and the imagination, especially art and literature, has always been a key element of control by dictators from both right and left when they take over countries. Books are burned, statues and paintings smashed, churches and temples destroyed, and the people who created or sustained them are killed or imprisoned.

Censors in our society attack books that require young readers to use their imagination because it encourages them to envision the world as something other than it is. That ability to imagine things new and different, however, is what is necessary for the development of thought, judgment, and creativity. An Illinois district court ruled against RR parents who objected to the *Impressions* series, noted previously. The judge stated that the books were not part of a "pagan religion" but were well-written fantasies that develop children's imaginations in ways important to their education and future lives: "What would become of elementary education, public or private, without works such as these and scores and scores of others that serve to expand the minds of young children and develop their sense of creativity?" (*Court Rules*, 1994).

To the RR, the most frightening elements in life are the imagination and subconscious, for what occurs there is usually random and chaotic, often unconventional, and sometimes bizarre. Teachers and parents cannot control even their own imaginations, let alone their children's. They can never know what is going on in the privacy of young minds while reading or writing, nor can they limit the thoughts that are evoked by words and images. So for those who believe that the minds and behaviors of students should be strictly controlled and severely limited, developing the imagination is perilous. They themselves, however, exhibit a great deal of imagination in their conspiracy theory about public education, the evil influence of widely praised books, and their frequent use of quotations from the Founding Fathers, such as Jefferson, Madison, Franklin, Washington, Adams, and Thomas Paine to support their right-wing fundamentalist Christian views.

A freely indulged imagination is for many people the basis for creativity and a source of hope and comfort. Sometimes it is the savior of sanity and life. Survivors of concentration camps and other inhumane environments have testified that the only way they bore up was to escape into the world of their imagination, the one place where freedom still lived. Thus, literature—created by free minds and contemplated in isolation—is the ultimate threat to the goal of mind control. The more unique and imaginative the work, the greater the threat.

Katherine Paterson (1981), author of *A Bridge to Terabithia* (a frequent target of censors), said, "The fake characters we read about will evaporate like the morning dew, but the real ones, the true ones, will haunt us for the rest of our days" (p. 59). These "true ones," of course, come out of the writer's imagination and reside in the reader's. Traits are selected, personalities combined, mannerisms and peculiarities exaggerated, time telescoped, until characters and events emerge that, although created by the writer, are true and real. Without imagination great literature as well as great discoveries and theories could not emerge, and those who read could not wander in the realm where freedom reigns and truth prevails.

Would we have a nation like ours if the imaginations of our forefathers for a new kind of government had been bounded? Would we have art, music, science, technology, medical cures, or even sports and business? Envisioning the new, going beyond the known, does not suddenly happen in adults when it has been repressed and denigrated in children. An active imagination is important in every field and it needs encouragement from the time children are tiny—and schools can and should play a big part in that. Imagination is essential to all learning, and reading and writing imaginative stories helps in its development.

In a personal note to readers, Daniel J. Boorstin wrote the following in his book *The Creators* (1992), which is a survey of the arts from ancient times to the present:

> These creators, makers of the new, can never become obsolete, for in the arts there is no correct answer. The story of the discoverers could be told in simple chronological order, since the latest science replaces what went before. But the arts are another story—a story of infinite addition. We must find order in the random flexings of the imagination...each of us alone must experience how the new adds to the old and how the old enriches the new, how Picasso enhances Leonardo and how Homer illuminates Joyce. (p. xv)

In a book called *The Craft of Poetry* (Packard, 1974), a series of interviews of contemporary poets, Stanley Kunitz said about poetry what could apply to any creative endeavor. "The work of the imagination is precisely what has to be achieved if we are going to save our civilization from disaster...a poem, regardless of its theme, can embody for us a principle of the free mind engaged in a free action" (p. 34). To engage students' free minds in free actions is the ultimate goal of education in our democracy.

II

RELIGION AND MORALITY IN SELECTED CHALLENGED LITERATURE

6

Religion and Morality
in Slaughterhouse-Five by Kurt
Vonnegut[1]

"Nothing intelligent to say about a massacre"

Slaughterhouse-Five, first published in 1966 during the Vietnam War, has been targeted for banning or burning ever since.[2] In 1973, for instance, three dozen paperback copies of the novel were burned by the school superintendent and board members in Drake, North Dakota, after a high school sophomore complained about the profanity (Veix, 1975). Two years earlier a circuit court judge in Michigan told an area high school to ban the book or he would order it done himself because it was a "degradation of the person of Christ" and full of "repetitive obscenity and immorality" (*Banning of Billy*, 1971, p. 681).

Examples of the attacks on *Slaughterhouse-Five* in the 1980s include the following: In Racine, Wisconsin, because of the "language used in the book, depictions of torture, ethnic slurs, and negative portrayals of women"; in LaRue County, Kentucky, because it "contains foul language and promotes deviant sexual behavior"; in Fitzgerald, Georgia, because it is "filled with profanity and full of explicit sexual references"; in Baton Rouge, Louisiana, for being "vulgar and offensive"; and in Monroe, Michigan, for the language and the way women are portrayed (Doyle, 1994, p. 65).

In the 1990s the book was challenged in Jackson Township, Ohio, for its profanity and sexual content; in Waterloo, Iowa, because certain passages might cause students to be embarrassed or insulted; and in Plummer, Idaho because of profanity (Foerstel, 1994, p. 190). In 1995, *Slaughterhouse-Five* was

---

[1]The page numbers for quotations are from the 1991 Laurel Book paperback edition, New York: Dell.

[2]See Veix (1975) for a good discussion of how to teach *Slaughterhouse-Five* to high-school students.

59

still on the National Council of Teachers of English (NCTE) list of top 10 literature books most censored in secondary schools.

On February 13 and 14, 1945, English and American forces bombed Dresden, the jewel city of eastern Germany. The attack lasted 14 hours and killed 135,000 persons (the Germans say 220,000).[3] It was the deadliest air attack of all time. In contrast, the American B-29 raid on Tokyo killed 83,000, and 71,000 perished after the atomic explosion in Hiroshima. More than two and a half times as many civilians died in the Dresden bombing and resultant firestorm as in Britain in all of World War II. It took 3 months to bury the dead, most of them in mass graves, burned beyond recognition.

A center for art, theater, and museums, Dresden was undefended, for it had no war industries or troop concentration, nothing of any value to the war effort. Certain that the city would not be harmed, the population swelled from 600,000 to 1.4 million as women, children, elderly men, handicapped, and war-wounded fled there to escape the advancing Russians.

At 10:00 on February 13, 244 British bombers dropped 650,000 incendiary bombs that turned the city into a holocaust. Three hours later a second wave of 529 British planes struck again in order to kill the firefighters, rescue workers, and fleeing inhabitants. The third strike on the 14th was by American bombers, who then flew under the smoke and strafed escaping refugees (including American POWs, among them Kurt Vonnegut). Not a single gun was fired at either the British or American planes. Hit especially hard was a railroad station filled with women, children, and the elderly, but no soldiers. Two trains of refugee children stood in an open yard outside the station. All were killed.

The city burned for 7 days and smoldered for weeks. The glow from the fires could be seen 200 miles away. Central heating systems burst, and basements where people hid from the bombs were filled with scalding water. Most died from burns, hot gases, carbon monoxide, and smoke poisoning. The temperature reached over 1,000° F in the firestorm, completely incinerating bricks and tiles as well as people. This firebombing of Dresden was kept a secret by the Allies for 23 years.

Why does the assigning of this book elicit such anger from some parents and administrators as well as RR leaders? In this chapter, as well as succeeding ones, we look briefly at claims made by would-be censors, mostly from the RR, that have been made against each book, followed by a counterargument. The claims are often made by parents sincerely concerned about protecting their children from words and ideas they believe evil and damaging. These fears are fueled by the extremist rhetoric of right-wing leaders who have as their goal the destruction of public education. The critics have the right to voice their opinions, and to ask for other

---

[3]The statistics are taken from David Irving's book, *The Destruction of Dresden* (1963).

selections for their own children, but teachers also have the right to defend and promote the works they believe will benefit students morally, academically, socially, and spiritually.

The counterarguments are presented, not as the only alternative views or the correct intellectual positions, but as suggestions for refuting the charges sometimes made against frequently selected literature. Also, the passages from both the literature books and the Bible are deliberately taken out of context because that is the method used to attack them. As stated before, I believe that the most effective way to confront the accusations of immorality and antireligion is to use the same tactics and sources as the most strident critics. Both teachers and students, in the process of democratic discussion and debate, however, have the freedom to agree or disagree with any or all of the ideas offered here for consideration and to put forth their own opinions on each of the controversial issues.

ISSUE: PATRIOTISM

THE CENSORS' CLAIM: The book is an indictment of war, criticizes government actions, is anti-American, and unpatriotic.

Controversial Segments

Kurt Vonnegut explained in the first chapter why he came to write *Slaughterhouse-Five*, which is subtitled, *The Children's Crusade: A Duty Dance with Death*. He was a POW during World War II and imprisoned in a slaughterhouse in Dresden the night it was firebombed. After the war, Vonnegut went to see an old war buddy to reminisce about those times before starting his new book. The friend's wife, Mary O'Hare, one of the persons to whom the book is dedicated, was angry about this visit and finally told him why. "You were just babies in the war—like the ones upstairs!...You'll be played in the movies by Frank Sinatra and John Wayne....And war will look just wonderful, so we'll have a lot more of them. And they'll be fought by babies like the babies upstairs" (p. 14). She wanted no more books that glorified war. Her children, she hoped, would grow up in a peaceful world where violence was not the method used by the powerful to overcome the enemy.

Vonnegut understood her revulsion and said that this book "is so short and jumbled and jangled...because there is nothing intelligent to say about a massacre. Everybody is supposed to be dead....Everything is supposed to be very quiet after a massacre, and it always is, except for the birds. And what do the birds say? All there is to say about a massacre, things like 'Poo-tee-weet?'" (p. 19).

COUNTERARGUMENT: The book is an indictment of war and criticizes government actions that were wrong and inhumane, but that does not make it unpatriotic.

Vonnegut painted a gruesome, graphic picture of what this particular military episode was like for those involved, and condemned England and America for the vicious and unnecessary attack on an unarmed city and its civilian population. No matter what atrocities Hitler and his henchmen were committing, the children, women, old men, and crippled people in Dresden, as well as the exquisite buildings and art, did not deserve such terrible death and destruction. The loving, caring Father found in the Bible does not order the massacre of innocents as retribution for the sins of their political leaders, but tells us to "do no violence" (Luke 3:14), to "love your enemies" (Matt. 5:44), and not "shed innocent blood" (Jer. 22:3).

In fact, according to theologian Daniel Maguire (1982), peace is the central theme of the New Testament and also of the teaching of the Hebrew prophets. For 300 years after the crucifixion of Jesus, the church was still pacifistic. Not until the reign of Constantine did it turn to war as a means of settling disputes and spreading Christianity (pp. 90–95).

Young people may refuse to serve in future combats after reading about the horrors of war in novels like *Slaughterhouse-Five*, as the RR fears, but this does not make them un-American. They do not want their country to engage in violence, to exterminate whole populations, but to find other ways to resolve conflicts. Students may rightfully rebel against mass killing as a viable solution to world problems. They may decide to "beat their swords into plowshares, and their spears into pruninghooks," to not "learn war any more" (Is. 2:4; Micah 4:3), and to "seek peace, and pursue it" (Ps. 34:14). They may, in short, take to heart the biblical message of harmony among peoples and nations and believe the statement attributed to Jesus that "blessed are the peacemakers" who will be "called the children of God" (Matt. 5:9).

ISSUE: DESCRIPTIONS OF SOLDIERS' LIVES AND LANGUAGE

THE CENSORS' CLAIM: The book is full of degrading depictions of wartime life and the foul language used by soldiers, which are totally inappropriate for adolescents to read.

Controversial Segments

Vonnegut reports that Roland Weary, the "stupid and mean" 18-year-old antitank gunner, had earlier fired a shot in anger that missed the enemy. It made "a ripping sound like the opening of the zipper on the fly of God Almighty" (p. 34). The Germans returned the fire, killing every one on the gun crew except Weary.

Another time, the young foot soldier Billy Pilgrim and several others are behind the German lines and being shot at during the Battle of the Bulge. Billy is 6 feet 3 inches tall and has never been given a helmet, weapon, boots, or overcoat. Dazed from cold, hunger, and sleeplessness, he stands politely in the road, giving the German marksman another chance to kill him, for that is how he understands the rules of the war game. "Get out of the road, you dumb motherfucker," growls Weary. "The last word," says Vonnegut, "was still a novelty in the speech of white people in 1944" and so astonished Billy that it woke him up and got him to safety (p. 34).

The American POWS who are taken to Dresden by German soldiers are treated inhumanely, miserable beyond belief. Weary is forced to trade his good boots for German clogs. In the march through Luxembourg to Germany, his feet chafe and blister and become "blood puddings" (p. 64). A few days later he dies from gangrene.

The prisoners are put in a tightly locked boxcar and left to sit for 2 days. There is no food or fuel, and air is limited and stale. The men excrete into their steel helmets, and the car is so crowded they have to take turns standing or lying down: "The legs of those who stood were like fence posts driven into a warm, squirming, farting, sighing earth" (p. 70).

When the POWs arrive in Dresden, the 100 Americans are taken to the fifth slaughterhouse, originally built as a holding pen for pigs, guarded by eight boys, old men, and badly wounded veterans from the Russian campaign. Fortunately for the POWs, it is the only safe place. After the incineration of the city, the Americans and their guards emerge from the meat locker that protected them. The walls are still there, but the windows and roof are gone. Only ashes and melted glass remain inside. Nowhere is there food or water, and everywhere are "little logs" lying around that had once been people (p. 179). For 2 days Billy has to dig in the ground for corpses. When the bodies begin to rot and liquify and stink, the soldiers cremate them where they are with flamethrowers (p. 214).

COUNTERARGUMENT: The language and scenes, although revolting to the senses, are necessary to make the author's point about the terribleness of war.

Yes, these passages are difficult for anyone to read, let alone experience, but that is exactly why Vonnegut wrote them. The book's critics, I believe, are not angered by dirty words nearly as much as by the depiction of war's horribleness. High-school students will not be corrupted by reading this book, but will benefit from learning that war is not fun and games. It involves blood, pain, gore, and death on both sides of the battle. The soldiers use profanity, but not nearly as much as in real life. The worst words come from Roland Weary, who is so obnoxious that the other characters in the story reject him. He certainly would not appeal as a role model to teenagers.

Compared to the sinfulness of the bombing of a beautiful, nonmilitary city and the gassing and burning of 135,000 civilian inhabitants, the vulgar words used in the book are innocuous. They are no worse than what is heard every day on television or in the hallways of middle and high schools in cities, suburbs, or small towns. These phrases are commonly used by soldiers everywhere, especially in times of stress and fear. They are not meant to blaspheme God or religion, but to relieve the pervasive, debilitating tension and terror. In this case, the offensive word saved Billy's life. As Kurt Vonnegut wrote in a letter to the Board of Education, Drake, North Dakota, when his novel was burned, "Those words really don't damage children much. It was evil deeds and lying that hurt us" (cited in Stern, 1994, p. 201).

Vonnegut could not get his point across about the reality and degradation of war without using such images and words. Which is more obscene, he suggests, the phrase that comes to Weary's mind to explain the terrible awesomeness of the gun's blast, or the fact that his missed shot, done with anger rather than common sense, resulted in the death of all his comrades?

The author describes these happenings graphically and uses the everyday language of foot soldiers, not to titillate or offend readers, but to get across the message that war, even when one's country is the winner, is not glorious, but a living hell for both the combatants and the civilians caught in the strife. High-school students, who may be called to combat in some future war, should not be shielded from the reality of what they may unfortunately have to face.

ISSUE: SCIENCE FICTION AND FANTASY

THE CENSORS' CLAIM: Assigning stories about reinvented history and fictional planets is a waste of time and unfair to students. They should be learning factual information and the skills needed for their future lives.

Controversial Segments

After Billy Pilgrim returns from the war, marries, has a family, and is a contributing member of the community, he becomes "unstuck in time" (p. 23) and travels uncontrollably back and forth among World War II, the 1960s, and his childhood. One day he is kidnapped by aliens and taken by spaceship to the fictional planet Tralfamadore. The inhabitants are 2 feet high, green, and "shaped like plumber's friends" (p. 26). They have no voice boxes and speak telepathically.

Three years after the war, before his trip to Tralfamadore, Billy was committed to a mental hospital. Nobody believed it had anything to do with the war, not even his roommate Eliot Rosewater, a former infantry captain turned alcoholic who was there because he found life meaningless after his combat experiences. Rosewater introduced Billy to the works of the fictional fantasy writer, Kilgore Trout. To allay their posttraumatic stress syndromes, both men try to "reinvent themselves and their universe" through this medium (p. 101).

Readers are told, for instance, that in 1932 Trout wrote a story predicting the widespread use of burning jellied gasoline as a war weapon. It would be dropped on human beings by airplanes, piloted by robots who, having no conscience, could not imagine what was happening to the people on the ground. The leading robot looked and acted like a person and even dated girls. But, because he had no conscience, nobody blamed him for dropping burning jelly on people. What they could not tolerate was his bad breath. When he cleared that up, he was welcomed as a human being (p. 168).

COUNTERARGUMENT: Imaginary history and fantasy worlds are not dangerous to students, but are a creative, engaging way to challenge them to think about individual and societal morality.

Take war, for instance. Because the Tralfamadorians appear so peaceful, Billy expects them to be shocked and baffled by the bombings and other kinds of murder on Earth, to be afraid that the Earthlings' advanced knowledge and application of science might eventually destroy the whole universe. However, they never mention it until he does. When asked what was the most valuable thing he learned in his space visit, Billy answers, "How the inhabitants of a whole planet can live in peace!" (p. 116). To his surprise, he is told that Tralfamadore, too, has had wars "as horrible as any you've ever seen or read about." But they are apathetic about the horrors. "There isn't anything we can do about them," one says, "so we simply don't look at them. We ignore them. We spend eternity looking at pleasant moments" and they urge him to do the same (p. 117).

This episode could be an excellent starting point for a class discussion about fatalism, whether war is sometimes necessary, if there are moral limits, and if apathy is a danger. The Trout story about the robot raises the ethical issue of Americans dropping burning jelly on Vietnamese villages. The use of a fictional culture reduces students' feelings about particular wars, where they may have experienced a family loss, and facilitates more abstract reasoning. The created history also invites questioning of our country's real-life actions, which teaches students a valuable lesson about democracy: We have the freedom to challenge authority, which is forbidden in theocracies and other dictatorships, and to demand that government officials tell the truth about their actions and be held responsible.

In the New Testament, Jesus often used stories to make his points, such as the Good Samaritan and the prodigal son. Science fiction was, of course, an unknown term and modern technology unimaginable in biblical days. However, one could say that Jonah in the whale, Moses parting the Red Sea, and Joshua stopping the sun were all science-fiction stories, not meant to be taken literally but to impress the listeners with God's power and the advantage of placing one's trust in supernatural guidance.

ISSUE: NUDITY AND SEX

THE CENSORS' CLAIM: The book contains scenes of both nudity and adultery. The inhabitants of the fictional planet may not be human, but watching captive nude humans urinate and fornicate is still voyeurism.

Controversial Segments

Billy Pilgrim and the history teacher Edgar Derby are taken to the kitchen upon their arrival at Slaughterhouse Five by a 16-year-old guard who has never been in the building before. He opens what he thinks is the kitchen door, but instead it is the door to a communal shower being used by 30 teenage girls, German refugees from Breslau who have just arrived from their burned-out city. The girls scream and cover themselves with their hands, making themselves "utterly beautiful" (p. 159). The men quietly close the door and move on.

After Billy arrives on Tralfamadore, he is put unclothed into a geodesic dome that simulates an Earthling habitat, while a guide explains his living habits to the tiny, "household plumber-shaped" inhabitants. When Billy goes to the bathroom, the spectators go wild. A nude 20-year-old movie star named Montana Wildhack is brought in and a huge crowd gathers to watch the two mate.

COUNTERARGUMENT: The scenes of nudity and sex are neither lewd nor lascivious. They make points important to the theme of the book and are handled with respect.

The American POWs later learn that the young females in the shower were placed in a shallower shelter in another part of the stockyards and all were killed by the Allied bombing. They also see the bodies of other girls caught outside in the firestorm, who tried to protect themselves by jumping into the water cistern and were boiled alive—an event corroborated in David Irving's, *The Destruction of Dresden* (1963). Thus, again, the author shows rather than tells what a horrible massacre the bombing was, what an inhumane wasting of young lives.

The sex scene with Billy and Montana is mentioned only briefly and without description. When Montana sees little green hands applauding, she screams, and a blue canopy is dropped over the dome for privacy. Lewd thoughts do not come to Billy's mind when he sees the girl's beautiful body, says the author. Instead he remembers Dresden's gorgeous architecture before it was destroyed by Allied bombers.

The fact that they are both on display to the inhabitants is a humorous comparison with our exhibition of animals in a zoo, especially visitors gawking at mating panda bears in Washington, DC. To the Tralfamadorians, the two humans are rare specimens that excite their curiosity, not their hormones. They are fascinated by the habits and lifestyles of these unique creatures which, of course, includes eating, elimination, and intercourse. No lascivious words are used and no descriptions of the sexual activities are given.

Because Billy is kidnapped, has no way to escape, and is given a lovely captive mate, he settles in to live his life as enjoyably as he can. Even if this is viewed as adultery and sinful, the New Testament reports that Jesus preached forgiveness of sins. For example, when a woman caught in adultery was about to be stoned, he called out, "He that is without sin among you, let him cast the first stone," and her attackers slunk away (John 8:7).

ISSUE: INTERPRETATIONS OF THE BIBLE AND CHRISTIANITY

THE CENSORS' CLAIM: The book is anti-Christian, atheistic, and blasphemous. It satirizes the New Testament, calls Jesus a *bum* and a *nobody*, and maintains that everything in life happens merely by chance rather than by God's will.

Controversial Segments

Billy, whose last name is Pilgrim, was a chaplain's assistant in the war—often a figure of fun for irreverent soldiers. He played hymns on a little black organ that was waterproof. He also had a portable altar. Inscribed on both was the name of the vacuum cleaner company that made them. Although Billy had "an extremely gruesome crucifix" (p. 38) hanging on the wall of his bedroom at home, he was not Catholic. His father was indifferent to religion. His mother was a substitute organist for several churches in town and took her son with her when she played. She claimed she would join a church when she decided which one was right, but never decided. She bought the crucifix on a trip to Santa Fe during the Depression.

Most of the direct references to religious belief come from Billy's experience after the war when he is captured by aliens and taken to the planet Tralfamadore. He is perplexed at being selected for this trip because he was never chosen for anything before. "Why me?" he asks his captor. "That is a very *Earthling* question to ask, Mr. Pilgrim. Why *you*? Why *us* for that matter? Why *anything*? Because this moment simply *is*. Have you ever seen bugs trapped in amber? . . . here we are, Mr. Pilgrim, trapped in the amber of this moment. There is no *why*" (pp. 76–77).

"Only on Earth," continues the Tralfamadorian, "is there any talk of free will." Instead of trying to explain everything, he says, one should just accept each moment as it is. "All time is all time. It does not change. It does not lend itself to warnings or explanations. It simply *is*. Take it moment by moment, and you will find that we are all, as I've said before, bugs in amber" (p. 86).

In a Kilgore Trout story, a visitor from outer space finds the Christian story absurd and gives an unusual interpretation of it. Jesus, he said, was a nobody and a pain in the neck to authorities who decided to get rid of him by nailing him to a cross, thinking there would be no repercussions. But just before the "nobody" died, God announced in a thunderous voice that he was "adopting the bum as his son, giving him the full powers and privileges of The Son of the Creator of the Universe throughout all eternity." Then God added: *"From this moment on, He will punish horribly anybody who torments a bum who has no connections!"* (pp. 109–110).

In another of Trout's stories, a man builds a time machine so he can go back to see Jesus. The experiment is successful and he observes Jesus when he was 12 years old, learning carpentry from his father. Two Roman soldiers come into the workshop with a drawing on papyrus of something they want built by sunrise. Jesus and his father, happy to have the work, build the cross and a rabble-rouser is executed (p. 202).

COUNTERARGUMENT: The book is not anti-Christian, atheistic, or blasphemous. It raises theological questions that are found in many religions, including Christianity, and amusingly shows how biblical passages can be interpreted in different ways.

"Authentic religion," wrote Rabbi Harold Kushner in *When All You've Ever Wanted Isn't Enough* (1986), "does not want obedient people. It wants authentic people, people of integrity. What is integrity? The word 'integral' means whole, undivided, all of one piece" (p. 132). Authentic religion does not expect us to be perfect, to simply follow rules, he said, but to be people who grow and learn and change and discover our best natures. "Religion should even encourage us to challenge its own positions critically" and "give us courage to find our own way" (p. 130). In other words, religion should not demand conformity of thought and rigid behaviors, but encourage people to encounter other belief systems and to question and test whatever one has been taught.

Noting how often religious convictions have been used as the basis for wars, enslavement, prejudicial laws, and other attacks on humanity, Maguire wrote that "when someone claims to represent Christianity, we must demand to know whether it is the horror or the inspiration they represent" (1982, p. 88).

Vonnegut explored such ideas by creating another Kilgore Trout book, called *The Gospel from Outer Space,* in which an alien visitor makes a serious study of why Christians find it so easy to be cruel. He concludes that part of the trouble is the "slipshod storytelling in the New Testament" and explains his incredulity: "The flaw in the Christ stories. . . was that Christ, who didn't look like much, was actually the Son of the Most Powerful Being in the Universe." So readers think, *"Oh, boy—they sure picked the wrong guy to lynch that time!* And that thought had a brother: *'There are* right people *to lynch.'* Who? People not well connected" (pp. 108–109).

The intent, the alien said, seemed to be to tell people to "be merciful, even to the lowest of the low. But the Gospels actually taught this: *Before you kill somebody, make absolutely sure he isn't well connected"* (pp. 108–109).

Those who do not understand or cannot tolerate satire about religion are outraged at any mocking of biblical passages or interpretations. They also exhibit much insecurity and lack of faith. Are they afraid the Son of God will destroy all who read these tongue-in-cheek anecdotes? Is that the Jesus of love and peace described in the New Testament? Does God the Father not understand or appreciate humor and whimsy, nor grasp the passionate concern for justice and equality that lies behind the irreverent words?

The preceding segments in Trout's fantasies illustrate how someone who has grown up in a different religion or none at all might view the Christian story quite differently from believers of that faith. Those who fear the wrath of an angry God, however, will probably find the alien's humorous view of the Jesus story threatening as well as offensive. But what, exactly, is a *bum?* One who wanders around with no means of support, has no job or money, accepts handouts, gets food and shelter wherever he can find it. And a *nobody?* Someone whose family has neither money nor prestige, who has made no great career achievement. Indeed, the New Testament Jesus fits both descriptions.

Readers, thus, are confronted with ideas they may not have heard before, which may challenge beliefs taught at home and church. Certainly the Tralfamadorian philosophy is provocative, but that is what reading and education are all about. World War II, which happened in the lifetime of many people living today, is a good focus for an in-class wrestling with religious and moral issues without imposing any particular dogma. Students can read books such as *The Diary of Anne Frank* and Elie Wiesel's *Night,* to learn of the Nazi atrocities on Jews and other victims, and *Slaughterhouse-Five* to discover what was done by the Allies to German civilians. We must all, at some time and on some level, confront the universal questions of why things happen, how much control—if any—humans have over daily happenings, whether there is a supernatural power guiding events or if they happen by mere chance, and whether humans can alter the course of history by conscious actions.

Were those imprisoned or gassed in German concentration camps selected by God to be in that place at that time? Were the German children who were burned to death or boiled alive in the Dresden holocaust specially chosen for this massacre? More recently in America, were those who died from the explosions of buildings and airplanes meant to be there, or were they just victims of bad luck?

Passages can be found in the Bible that speak of a *chosen people* who will be rewarded for good behavior or right belief, and wicked people who will be punished, but the New Testament speaks of God's impartiality: "He maketh His sun to rise on the evil and on the good, and sendeth rain on the just and on the unjust" (Matt. 5:45), and the Book of Acts states that "God is no respecter of persons" (10:34). In *When Bad Things Happen to Good People*, Kushner (1989), whose son died at age 14 after a lifetime of suffering from a congenital disease, rejected the belief that the terrible things that happen in people's lives are God's punishment. He wrote:

> God does not cause our misfortunes. Some are caused by bad luck, some are caused by bad people, and some are simply an inevitable consequence of our being human and being mortal, living in a world of inflexible natural laws. The powerful things that happen to us are not punishments for our misbehavior, nor are they in any way part of some grand design on God's part....We can turn to Him for help in overcoming [a tragedy], precisely because we can tell ourselves that God is as outraged by it as we are. (p. 134)

Reading books such as *Slaughterhouse-Five* demonstrates to students that there are numerous beliefs concerning the meaning of life, death, and suffering, some of which are diametrically opposed. No matter how firmly one believes a particular viewpoint to be *God's truth*, the fact remains that alternate views are also strongly held by others equally convinced. Students will come across at least some of these in their lifetime, and many if they go to a nonfundamentalist college. Banning this book or others will not shelter them from ideas contrary to those of either mainstream or right-wing Christian interpretations.

RR believers are incensed by any challenge to their interpretations and especially to Vonnegut's sardonic views of orthodoxy. In a classroom, their children as well as others should have the opportunity to share their religious beliefs when appropriate to the context, but teachers do not have the obligation to shield them from other viewpoints. A major purpose of education in a democracy is for students to have access to reliable information and a variety of opinions, and not be forced into conformity of thought. Beliefs concerning religious issues are sometimes pertinent topics for class discussions and should not be excluded from the marketplace of ideas or limited to anyone's idea of *the one true faith*.

Moreover, whether Kurt Vonnegut is an atheist or personally believes the Tralfamadorians' philosophy of life is immaterial. Students will gain from, rather than be harmed by, a meeting of religious views different from their own. Like Jesus who, according to the New Testament, challenged the religious orthodoxy of his day—gathering food and healing the sick on the Sabbath (Matt. 12:1–14) and scolding the Pharisees for loud, ostentatious prayers (Matt. 6:5–6)—the views of various characters in a novel will stimulate thought and an evaluation of beliefs that may lead students to a firmer, more mature, more authentic faith.

7

Religion and Morality in The Catcher in the Rye by J. D. Salinger[1]

"That's the thing I'd really like to be"

For many years the book that headed the list of challenged literature was Salinger's *The Catcher in the Rye*, the classic story of a teenager's quest for maturity. Although other works have recently filled the top spot, *Catcher* is still a book the RR loves to hate. "Obscene" is the usual cry, based on the use of four-letter words. "Blasphemous" they claim because of the boy's caustic comments about religious hypocrisy. *Catcher* is a symbol for what RR critics perceive to be a plot on the part of teachers to undermine the morals of American school children.

Published in 1951, the book quickly found a receptive audience and landed on *The New York Times* best-seller list. Controversy over its use in classrooms and availability in libraries erupted from the beginning and still occurs, but readers continue to find a kindred soul in the protagonist Holden Caulfield, whose naive but honest statements express their own thoughts and feelings about such things as hypocrisy, sex, death, and religion.

The first recorded attempts to censor the book were in California in 1954, followed by eight more nationwide the following year. By 1981, *Catcher* had become one of the most frequently taught books in public high schools and the most frequently censored, according to Herbert Foerstel in *Banned in the U.S.A.* (1994, p. 146).

In the 1990s, challenges to the work have been made in such states as Maryland, South Carolina, Idaho, Oregon, California, and Pennsylvania. In Leesburg, Florida, in 1991 would-be censors wanted the book removed from the school library because of "profanity, reference to suicide, vulgarity, disrespect, and anti-Christian sentiments" that would lead teenagers to

---

[1]Page numbers for quotations are from the Signet Book paperback edition, New York: New American Library of World Literature, 6th printing, 1957.

"rebellion," "despair," and "low self-esteem." They objected to scenes that included alcohol consumption and smoking and claimed that "every page is filled with pessimism, profanity, poor attitudes and vulgarism" (Foerstel, 1994, p. 149).

A parent in Waterloo, Iowa, in 1992 objected to "too much swearing, repeated [use of] God's name in vain, and remarks about Jesus Christ," which would increase the use of bad language among teenagers, "turn kids off to religion" and encourage them "to think about sex" (Foerstel, 1994, p. 150). Several parents in Sidell, Illinois, in 1992 protested the book's use in a twelfth-grade English class because of "alleged obscenity, profanity, immorality, and references to premarital sex, alcohol abuse, and prostitution" (p. 149).

The Catcher in the Rye focuses on the lifestyle and problems of the well-to-do Caulfield family in New York City in 1947, when the end of World War II brought economic prosperity to those in professional careers. Money has not shielded them from sickness and heartbreak, however. The father is a corporate lawyer, the mother a housewife, the eldest son writes short stories and plays in California, 10-year-old Phoebe is a star pupil in elementary school, and the protagonist Holden is a 17-year-old student at an expensive boys' college prep school. The youngest son Allie died the year before of leukemia. Despite the family's attempt to continue their usual lives and maintain family cohesiveness, the illness and death of Allie has clearly had its emotional impact. The one most severely affected is Holden.

The parents, although loving and concerned about their children's well-being, are involved in many outside activities. A housekeeper is employed to do daily chores and to babysit Phoebe. The children are intelligent, talented, and (except for Holden) ambitious—the kind of offspring that make parents proud. Other than literature and writing, however, Holden takes no interest in school subjects, puts forth little effort, considers himself the dumb one in the family, and has moved from school to school to no avail.

In this first-person narration of his feelings and troubles, Holden emerges as a confused adolescent loved by his family and liked by teachers, peers, girlfriends, and even total strangers, despite the problems he creates for himself and others. He lacks ambition, but has charm. He considers many people *phony*, but is often generous and kind. Teetering between self-destruction and survival, Holden finally yields to the love of his little sister and acquires the help he needs for his psychological breakdown.

ISSUE: ROLE MODELING

THE CENSORS' CLAIM: The main character, Holden Caulfield, is an obnoxious, self-absorbed, lazy, ungrateful twerp with a foul mouth and

negative attitude. He is irresponsible, immature, and a liar—a terrible role model for teenagers.

Controversial Segments

The story opens with Holden skipping a football game at his elite boys' school. Thanksgiving vacation is near and he has learned he must leave school after Christmas because of failing grades. He also has other problems. The fencing team, which he managed, went into New York City for a meet that morning, only to forfeit the game because Holden accidently left all the foils and equipment on the subway. The next evening he suddenly decides to leave the school before the term ends and go to New York City, where he wanders around aimlessly for several days, spending money his wealthy grandmother has sent him, instead of going home.

Only 16 when he entered the school, Holden was already smoking cigarettes and, although forbidden, still smokes in his dorm room after others are asleep. He has failed four out of five classes, despite repeated warnings from his teachers. He admits to his teacher that he only glanced though his history text the whole term and that he has few concerns for his future. In fact, this is the fourth school he has gone to. Holden blatantly tells his readers, "I'm the most terrific liar you ever saw in your life. It's awful. If I'm on my way to the store to buy a magazine, even, and somebody asks me where I'm going, I'm liable to say I'm going to the opera" (p. 18). By his own admission, he sometimes acts "like I'm about thirteen" (p. 12).

COUNTERARGUMENT: Holden is a confused teenager searching for self-worth and values. His words often belie the responsible, moral behavior he exhibits.

Although Holden is failing classes because he does not apply himself and claims he is illiterate, he voluntarily reads classical literature. His favorite authors, besides his brother who writes short stories, are Ring Lardner, Thomas Hardy, Isak Dineson, and Somerset Maugham. He also reads war books and mysteries, but isn't as impressed with those. "What really knocks me out," he says, "is a book that, when you're all done reading it, you wish the author...was a terrific friend of yours" (p. 20). Unlike many students who read superficially only what is assigned, Holden eagerly devours books and makes them part of his life. He does well in English class and understands that good writing comes from the heart and touches both the writer and reader.

Holden admits to lying, but his motives are usually to protect others' feelings or to get out of awkward situations. He doesn't want to tell his elderly teacher the true reasons for ending the visit, so he makes up a plausible excuse to exit gracefully. Don't most of us do the same in uncomfortable situations? Later he tells a woman he meets on the train that he is going home early to have an operation on "this tiny little tumor on the brain" and that he can't visit her son, whom he detests, because he is going to South America with his grandmother (p. 55). His lies are either well intentioned or harmless and often absurdly amusing.

This teenager is going through a phase that confronts many young adults. As the psychologist Erik Erikson (1968) showed, adolescence is the time for breaking away from family, gradually assuming independence, finding oneself. Holden, who is sensitive and perceptive, lives in the shadow of a talented older brother and is still mourning the death of the one 2 years younger. He is not a lazy, self-centered oaf, but has found it impossible to concentrate on studies and has a negative view of the world—typical signs of severe depression. He suffers from a poor self-image and has not yet found his inner spirit, his true self. As the Bible says, "Thou shalt love thy neighbor *as thyself*" [italics added] (Lev. 19:18, Matt. 19:19). Holden does not at this point love himself, but is seeking to escape from deep feelings of inferiority and a belief that he has let his family down.

ISSUE: HYPOCRISY

THE CENSORS' CLAIM: Holden is disrespectful of authority and believes most people, except himself, are *phonies.*

Controversial Segments

Holden criticizes the wealthy funeral director who provided a new dormitory, calling him a phony, as he does most males. A graduate of the school, the donor gave a long speech in chapel claiming that whenever he was in trouble, he got down on his knees and prayed to God. They should all look upon Jesus as their friend: "He said *he* talked to Jesus all the time. Even when he was driving his car. That killed me. I can just see the big phony bastard shifting into first gear and asking Jesus to send him a few more stiffs" (pp. 18–19).

Instead of going to the football field, Holden goes to see his ailing history teacher who has written a note asking to see him before he leaves school. The man was "old as hell" and "if you thought about him *too* much, you wondered what the heck he was still living for. I mean he was all stooped over, and he had a very terrible posture" (p. 10). Holden says he could converse with the man and think about other things at the same time, such as the ducks in the lagoon in Central Park, because "you don't have to think too hard when you talk to a teacher" (p. 15).

COUNTERARGUMENT: Holden is very respectful to those he feels deserve it, and has good reasons for criticizing the others.

Yes, Holden hates *phoniness*, which he finds in abundance in school administrators, visiting speakers, and many of his male classmates. According to Rabbi Harold Kushner (1986), who has counseled many youths, teenagers in general are quick to denounce hypocrisy in the adults around them. "One of the most dismissive names they can call someone is a 'phony,' a person who says things he or she does not mean or who claims to believe certain things but acts differently . . . hypocrisy and integrity are big issues for them during their formative years" (pp. 133–134).

Most of the females Holden encounters and all of the children, however, escape this condemnation. He likes the headmaster's daughter because "she didn't give you a lot of horse manure about what a great guy her father was. She probably knew what a phony slob he was" (p. 7).

The boy realizes his teacher will lecture him about not fulfilling his potential, and he doesn't like seeing old men in their pajamas with "their bumpy old chests" and their legs "so white and unhairy" (p. 10). Even though he knows that "old Spencer" (an affectionate term) will lecture him about failing his class, Holden goes to see the infirm, elderly man out of respect for a person who cares about his subject and his students. Despite his discomfort, Holden listens politely to the teacher's chastisement and the reading of the pitifully inadequate history essay he wrote on the last test. At the end of the paper, Holden had added an apology to Spencer for doing poorly, "so he wouldn't feel too bad about flunking me" (p. 15). For a 17-year-old to worry about an elderly teacher's feelings is moral behavior. To visit the sick man is even more so.

Holden hates hypocrisy. Like Jesus in the New Testament who was incensed over the behavior of the scribes and pharisees (Matt. 6:5), *Catcher's* main character rails against those who behave one way in public and another in private. He claims he left his last school because of the behavior of the headmaster, who would politely shake hands with a boy's mother who was "fat or corny-looking," but would spend half an hour with well-to-do, attractive parents (p. 16).

Holden objects to the catalogue at Pencey, which shows a student on a horse jumping over a fence and praises the "splendid, clear-thinking young men" the school produces. According to Holden, the school did not even own a horse, and the students were anything but splendid (p. 6). He believes the school serves steak on Saturday nights so Sunday's visiting parents will think the meals are always like that (pp. 34-35). Holden sees the school as manufacturing a public image that belies reality, a situation not uncommon with educational institutions.

One of the boy's most endearing qualities is his caring behavior toward people whom others shun. For instance, everybody hates Ackley. Besides snoring loudly, he has "sinus trouble, pimples, lousy teeth, halitosis, crumby fingernails." But, says Holden, "You had to feel a little sorry for the crazy sonuvabitch"(p. 38). He, however, is the only one who does. Although Ackley irritates him, Holden never turns him away. He makes snide remarks but he does not reject. He invites Ackley to go to a movie because he knows the boy has no other friends. With Ackley, as with others, *Catcher's* hero shows a concern not common with his peers.

Holden is especially distressed at the insensitivity of his classmates. He remembers a small, quiet student who refused to apologize for calling another fellow conceited. Six dormmates descended on his room. That night, wearing a green turtleneck sweater borrowed from Holden, he threw himself out the window. Holden still winces at the image of the boy sprawled dead on the sidewalk and thinks the harassers deserved more for their actions than school expulsion (p. 154).

Holden's understanding of the hypocrisy prevalent in the wealthy society that surrounds him and his solicitous behavior toward his elderly teacher and the outcasts in his school represent moral behavior that far surpasses that of many teenagers and adults.

ISSUE: PROFANITY

THE CENSORS' CLAIM: This book is so filled with filthy language, it should be burned.

Controversial Segments

There are in the book, according to several objectors who did careful tabulations, 860 obscenities, 785 profanities, and 295 instances of God's name taken in vain (Foerstel, 1994, p. 147). Typical examples are, "Goddam book," "For Chrissake, grow up," and "The hell he did, the bastard."

Near the end of the book, when Holden goes to Phoebe's elementary school to give her a note saying that he is leaving town, Holden sees *Fuck you* written on the wall. Going down another staircase, he finds it again, scratched on with a sharp instrument. He feels hopeless and says that in a million years it would be impossible to rub out even half of such signs in the world (pp. 181–182).

Holden goes to the Museum of Art to wait for Phoebe and right under the stones of the Egyptian tombs he sees another *Fuck you*, this time written with a red crayon. He says that when he dies he is positive that his tombstone will give his name and date of birth and death, and then "right under that it'll say 'Fuck you'" (p. 184).

COUNTERARGUMENT: Words by themselves are neutral and not corrupting, especially ones that carry little or no religious or sexual connotation for most young people today.

The context is what is important. Although some people still find these words offensive, they have become so commonplace for the younger generation that they have little meaning or power. In fact, seeing them repeated so often in this story loses its shock value very quickly. The reader soon learns that Holden has a limited, immature vocabulary and the words are mostly fillers for feelings he can't express. Holden does not mean to be blasphemous by saying *chrissakes* or *goddam* or *hell*. They are just phrases that show irritation, like *dog-gone-it* or *goldarn* or *heck*, which even fundamentalists use for the same purpose. It has nothing to do with religious belief or God. A loving heavenly Father would understand the confusion and needs of a mixed-up, depressed teenager and forgive this adolescent affectation.

In using the F-word, Salinger shows us most of all what a moral kid Holden truly is. When he sees the phrase written on the school wall, he goes crazy. He thinks of how his little sister Phoebe and the other children will wonder what it means. He wants to kill whoever wrote the words, to smash his head against the stone steps. He rubs the words off with his hands, afraid somebody will think *he* wrote them (p. 181). He feels helpless when he finds the phrase scratched on the stairwell wall and in amongst the museum display. These scenes illustrate Holden's desire to protect children from getting a "cockeyed" version of sex from "some dirty kid" (p. 181). Obviously sex for him is not an obscenity but an act of love between two people who respect each other. He does not use the word himself anywhere in the book and is upset that others spoil places that are "nice and peaceful" with words that society has deemed offensive (pp. 183–84).

ISSUE: SEXUAL THOUGHTS AND BEHAVIOR

THE CENSORS' CLAIM: The book describes sex between teenagers and a scene with a prostitute. Both are sinful, a humanist attempt to undermine the sacredness of marriage and the family.

Controversial Segments

A girl Holden knows from a pleasant summer vacation has a date with his roommate, a handsome, unscrupulous, self-centered, "sexy bastard." Holden sits worrying until they return, then starts a fistfight with the other boy for the indecent behavior he imagines has taken place. Most of his classmates talk about having sex with girls, he says, but Stradlater actually has done it. He fears for Jane's safety (p. 34).

Afraid to go home, Holden gets a hotel room in New York, and in the elevator is approached by a pimp who persuades him to "have a good time," which he decides to do. Before the girl arrives, he nervously brushes his teeth and changes his shirt. When she knocks on the door, he trips over his suitcase getting to it. She isn't any older than he—a skinny little thing with a high, squeaky voice. He hangs her dress in the closet so it won't wrinkle, then tries to make casual conversation, feeling "much more depressed than sexy." When she approaches with serious intentions, he panics, tells her he has just had an operation, apologizes profusely, and pays her $5 to leave (pp. 87–90).

COUNTERARGUMENT: Holden Caulfield is a confused but chaste young man who wants to save sex for marriage.

Purity is stressed as "blessedness" in the Bible (Matt. 5:8) and Holden is a good example of a teenager who resists the temptations. He is a virgin. He tells us that right off. Despite all the thoughts typical of an adolescent, and "quite a few opportunities," he has set a limit. As he puts it, in his mind he's "the biggest sex maniac you ever saw," but when he thinks about doing "crumby stuff" he doesn't like the idea. "Sex is something I really don't understand too hot" (pp. 58–59). When a girl tells him to stop, he says, he stops. He never wants to hurt or offend (p. 85).

Although he succumbs to the idea of having paid sex, just for the experience, Holden cannot go through with it. As the above controversial passage indicates, he clearly is not ready to lose his virginity and certainly not with a prostitute. The poignant scene dispels any belief that the young man is anything but a mixed-up adolescent with a strong sense of values.

Far from advocating illicit sex, the book discourages teenage readers from engaging in sexual relations either with prostitutes or dates. As Amitai Etzioni (1996), director of George Washington University's Center for Communitarian Policy Studies, said in an article about character education in public schools, "Removing *Catcher in the Rye*...from the school library will 'only' leave our children exposed to much more sexually explicit messages from magazines, movies, television, clothing stores, and the rest of our culture, including of course the Song of Songs, among other Biblical narratives" (p. 40).

ISSUE: HOMOSEXUALITY

THE CENSORS' CLAIM: Talking about homosexuality and including a scene, especially with a well-liked teacher, will make teenagers want to experiment with this perversity, which is a terrible sin, condemned repeatedly in the Bible. "A homosexual violates God's clearly prescribed will, thwarts his purpose for man, and has incurred 'the wrath of God'" (T. LaHaye, 1980, p. 11).

Controversial Segments

Late at night in a bar in a swanky hotel, Holden runs into a former schoolmate, now attending another school, who claims to know all about sex, especially homosexuality. He recounts to Holden all the famous people in the United States he is sure are gay or lesbian and tells him that a person can turn into a homosexual overnight (pp. 129–130).

When despair overtakes him, Holden slips into his parents' house and talks for a while to his affectionate little sister. He then goes to the home of a married former English teacher he especially liked to tell them about his troubles. After giving the boy some good advice about living humbly for a worthy cause and applying himself in school, Mr. Antolini invites Holden to spend the night and makes up the couch. "Good night, handsome," he says as he exits to his bedroom. Holden falls asleep, then is brought sharply awake by a strange feeling. The man is sitting on the floor in the dark, patting him on the head. Mumbling that he must get his bags that were left at the station, Holden quickly pulls on his clothes and heads for the elevator. He is shaken: "When something perverty like that happens, I start sweating like a bastard. That kind of stuff's happened to me about twenty times since I was a kid. I can't stand it" (p. 174).

COUNTERARGUMENT: Homosexuality is not a choice, but something one is born to be. Reading about it in a novel is not going to change anyone's sexual orientation.

Actually, the ones who should object to these passages are gays and lesbians who are demeaned by both "old Luce" and Holden as "perverts" instead of ordinary people who love someone of the same rather than opposite sex. In the New Testament, Jesus preaches love, tolerance, and acceptance. Today, much more than in the 1940s and 1950s, homosexuality is viewed by many in our society and in our churches as a normal lifestyle for consenting adults and not as a sin.

Teachers, whether straight or gay, must not use the classroom to discuss or promote their sexual preferences or behavior. It is as immoral and illegal to recruit opposite-gender students as same-gender ones, and those few who do either should rightfully be punished for harassment and child abuse. Most homosexual teachers are moral, honest folk who would not think of using their position in this manner. Their primary responsibility, as with all instructors, is to teach subject matter, thinking skills, and citizenship, and that is what they do.

If Mr. Antolini's behavior was indeed a sexually motivated act, then Holden was right in getting out of the apartment quickly. In fact, the boy's action in this case could serve as an example of what to do if a student is caught in such a situation. Young people *are* preyed on by some immoral people. Reading about this in a book such as *Catcher* can alert them to the danger and give them the wisdom and courage to protect themselves.

However, Holden had second thoughts once he left. Perhaps the teacher was just being kind and concerned. After all, the boy was in bad shape both physically and psychologically. It might have been a fatherly gesture, meant to soothe, not seduce. Holden remembers that when the boy in his dorm jumped to his death after being harassed by classmates, Mr. Antolini was the only teacher with the courage and compassion to pick up the broken body and carry it gently to the hospital. Besides, he had offered Holden comfort and wisdom for a troubled soul.

ISSUE: FAMILY VALUES

THE CENSORS' CLAIM: The main character criticizes his parents, which will encourage teenage readers to do the same, undermining parental authority and promoting disrespect.

Controversial Segments

Holden implies that his mother is an unhappy woman. He says, "You can hit my father over the head with a chair and he won't wake up, but . . . all you have to do to my mother is cough somewhere in Siberia and she'll hear you. She's nervous as hell" (p. 143). He claims that she is often up half the night smoking cigarettes, seems not to enjoy herself socially, and frequently has headaches.

Holden criticizes his father's legal vocation, which provides a high standard of living for the family. When his little sister asks if he wants to be a lawyer like his father, Holden replies that all lawyers do is make a lot of money, buy expensive cars, play golf and bridge, drink Martinis, and look like "hot-shots" (p. 155).

COUNTERARGUMENT: No teenager could demonstrate more love and respect for his family than Holden Caulfield.

Despite his caustic comments about lawyers and the observation that his mother is not happy, Holden loves his parents and siblings. He admires his father's abilities, his mother's taste in clothes and decorating, and his older brother's skill as a writer in Hollywood. He especially shows affection for his 10-year-old sister, Phoebe: "You never saw a little kid so pretty and smart in your whole life . . . if you tell old Phoebe something, she knows exactly what the hell you're talking about . . . you can even take her anywhere with you" (pp. 62–63).

Tragedy struck the Caulfield family a few years earlier when the third son, Allie, 2 years younger than Holden, died of leukemia. "You'd have liked him," says Holden. "He was the most intelligent member of the family. He was also the nicest" (p. 37). When Allie died, Holden went out to the garage and smashed all the windows with his bare hands.

Catcher's leading character is not rebelling against parental values. He is roaming the streets of New York because he wants to protect his family from the hurt he thinks his failure will bring. In the end, it is his love for his sister, and her love for him, that ends his escapades. He refuses to let Phoebe go with him on his runaway trip out West and takes her to the park to ride the carousel, then promises to go home afterward. It starts to rain hard as Phoebe goes round and round, but Holden doesn't care. "I felt so damn happy all of a sudden....I was damn near bawling, I felt so damn happy" (p. 191). His family lovingly welcomes him home and gets him the therapy he so obviously needs.

ISSUE: RELIGIOUS BELIEFS

THE CENSORS' CLAIM: The book is atheistic and blatantly attacks Christianity. Teachers have no right to use literature to promote their religion of secular humanism and denounce other faiths.

Controversial Segments

Holden says he is "sort of an atheist." His parents are from different religions and the family never goes to church. He claims he likes Jesus, but not the Disciples, who were not much use while Jesus was alive and just kept letting him down. Holden used to get into arguments with a Quaker schoolmate about the Disciples and whether or not Judas went to Hell after his betrayal. He says he would bet a thousand bucks, if he had that much, that Jesus would not have sent Judas to Hell, although the other Disciples would have (pp. 91–92).

When in New York City, Holden invites an old girlfriend to see the Christmas program at Radio City Hall. It is a religious theme, but Holden does not see anything religious or inspirational in a bunch of actors carrying crucifixes around the stage. "You could tell they could hardly wait to get a cigarette or something." If Jesus had seen all those fancy costumes, says Holden, he "probably would've puked" (p. 125).

COUNTERARGUMENT: Holden has great respect for those who are sincere in their faith, whatever it is.

He enjoys talking to two friendly nuns with cheap suitcases who sit next to him at the train lunch counter, teachers on their way to a new placement. He insists on giving them $10 as a contribution and, grateful that they didn't ask if he were Catholic, wishes he had given them more. Their humility and gentleness epitomize for him what religion should be (pp. 100–103). In contrast, the show-biz religion at Radio City Hall he finds repugnant. If Jesus were wholly man as well as wholly God, he quite likely would have been nauseated at the expensive, gaudy display. Holden dislikes the Disciples because of their faithlessness when danger arose. Loyalty for him is a very strong value, for his own predicament stems from the belief that he is letting down his family and is unworthy of their love.

ISSUE: ATTITUDE TOWARD LIFE

THE CENSORS' CLAIM: Holden is a sick, immature, suicidal adolescent who should be in a mental institution, where he evidently ends up.

Controversial Segments

Holden is clearly depressed and exhibits a very negative attitude about the life he is living. He says he hates school, living in New York, riding taxicabs and buses, going down an elevator to get outside (pp. 118–119). At one point he briefly contemplates suicide, but is stopped by the thought of people "looking at me when I was all gory" (p. 96). Later he says that he is glad the atomic bomb was invented and if there is another war he will volunteer to sit right on top of the bomb.

COUNTERARGUMENT: Holden is experiencing severe depression. At heart he is a compassionate, generous, moral young man who is truly fond of children and wants to save them from the phoniness and foulness he has found in the grown-up world.

While wandering around New York, Holden spies a poor family going home from church. A small boy is walking in the street singing the Scottish ditty, "Comin' Through the Rye." Holden later tells Phoebe that what he'd like to be more than anything else in the world is a "catcher in the rye." He pictures a large field with thousands of little kids playing and nobody big around but him. He stands at the edge of a steep cliff and catches the kids before they fall over. "I know it's crazy, but that's the only thing I'd really like to be" (p. 156). When his little sister offers him her Christmas money for his runaway trip, he starts to cry and weeps quietly for a long time (p. 162).

The New Testament states that one must become like a little child before one can enter the Kingdom of God (Mark 10:14, Luke 18:17). The innocence and simplicity of children also holds a special appeal for Holden. He demonstrates repeatedly his love for his younger sister. He empathizes with a little boy in a movie whose mother will not take him to the bathroom. He shows two young brothers how to find the mummies in the public museum, and helps a little girl tighten her ice skates in the park.

In this sometimes funny, sometimes painful, novel of a teenager's search for self-worth and values, Holden uses words typical of an insecure young man trying to appear grown-up. He tries out sexual ventures, only to retreat when he oversteps his moral limits. He drinks to escape the fear of hurting his family and falls into depression. None of this is painted as glamorous. None is likely to entice readers to go and do likewise.

Holden Caulfield is a confused but moral person. He befriends the friendless and respects those who are humble, loyal, and kind. He demonstrates a strong love for his family. He abhors hypocrisy. He values sex that comes from caring for another person and rejects its sordidness. Finally, he wants to be a responsible member of society, to guide and protect those younger than he. What greater morality can one want from a novel?*

---

*A shorter version of this chapter was published in 1983 as "What's moral about 'The catcher in the rye'?" *English Journal* 72(4), 39–42.

8

Religion and Morality in Of Mice and Men by John Steinbeck[1]

"We got each other"

In recent years, Steinbeck's 1937 classic *Of Mice and Men* rose to the top of the most challenged books in American schools from 1982 to 1995 (*Attacks on*, 1995, appendices, no page). Although this story about hope and love in the midst of misery still has the power to move first-time readers to tears, it also moves would-be censors to complain about profanity, prejudice, irreligion, and euthanasia. In 1994–1995, for instance, from Loganville, Georgia, to Bemidji, Minnesota, to Galena, Kansas, parents requested the book be removed from classroom reading lists and library shelves (*Attacks on*, pp. 85, 129, 103).

The school superintendent in Cookeville, Tennessee, who admitted not having read *Of Mice and Men*, pronounced, "Due to the language in it, we just can't have this kind of book being taught" (*Attacks on*, 1995, p. 27). In Loganville, Georgia, a parent who thumbed through the book rather than reading it demanded its removal because it was "laced with vulgarities and profanity" (p. 85).

In 1992, parents in Hamilton, Ohio, objected to the book because of its supposed anti-Christian content, vulgarity, profanity, and racial slurs. A minister pronounced, "Anybody that's got a child shouldn't want them to read this book. It should be burned up, put in a fire. . . . It's not fit for a heathen to read" (cited in Foerstel, 1994, p. 146). In 1991 an Iowa City, Iowa, mother claimed, "I feel my daughter was subjected to psychological and emotional abuse when the book was read aloud" (cited in Foerstel, p. 144). She didn't want her child talking like a migrant worker, she added. The book was removed (although later returned) from the reading list in

---

[1]Pages for quotations are taken from *The Short Novels of John Steinbeck*. New York: Viking Press. 1953.

Suwannee, Florida, in 1991 because it is "indecent" and puts "trash" in the children's minds (cited in Foerstel, p. 145).

Yet the book remains a popular text in high-school English classes and is strongly supported by many educators, parents, and ministers. Noting the contemporary prevalence of the homeless amidst a world of wealth, poet and novelist Jay Parini (1992) wrote in a *New York Times* article about the 1992 film version of *Of Mice and Men*, starring Gary Sinise and John Malkovich, that the novel and movie speak "to the condition of these homeless, powerless and neglected people in a manner that compels us to look again at their plight in wonderment and pity" (p. 24H).

Born into a middle-class family in Salinas, California, Steinbeck's mind and heart were captured as a young man by the tragedy of those during the 1930s Depression who had no material comforts, were beaten down time after time, yet managed to retain dignity, pride, and dreams. As Parini said about this novel, "*Of Mice and Men* moves with the inexorability of a huge river, and it pours itself, exhausts itself, in the sea of our unconscious. Having read it, we carry the book inside us forever" (p. 24H).

Steinbeck's stories are filled, not with perfect people, but with those who are dispossessed, who live at the edge of society, yet who survive and cling to life, no matter how painful the present or dismal the future. They exist on hope and occasional gifts of friendship, and the stronger characters exhibit love, compassion, and mercy to those who are weaker or worse off than they.

In an interview with *The New York Times* in 1937, Steinbeck explained the origins of the story:

> I was a bindlestiff [hobo] myself for quite a spell. I worked in the same country that the story is laid in. The characters are composites to a certain extent. Lennie was a real person. He's in an insane asylum in California right now. I worked alongside him for many weeks. He didn't kill a girl. He killed a ranch foreman. Got sore because the boss had fired his pal and stuck a pitchfork right through his stomach. I hate to tell you how many times I saw him do it. We couldn't stop him until it was too late. (cited in Parini, 1992, p. 24H)

Despite the 50 plus years since the novel's publication, it continues to stir our emotions, speculated Parini, because "something whispers to us that the Georges and Lennies...are not that far away" (p. 24H).

ISSUE: LANGUAGE

THE CENSORS' CLAIM: The book is filled with vulgar, profane words. They begin on the second page and never stop. Students should not be presented with such filthy language.

Controversial Segments

George, for instance, says the following during their escape from the law after Lennie has frightened a woman at their last job, "God damn near four miles, that's what it was!"..."Jesus Christ, you're a crazy bastard!"..."The hell with rabbits" (p. 158). One parent who counted said that "'G.D' is used 24 times and in other forms it is used 45 times....In 104 pages, I think, there are 108 profane words other than 'G.D'" (*Attacks on*, 1995, p. 85).

COUNTERARGUMENT: For a story to be authentic, authors must use the language characters would use in real life. Students will not be harmed by the speech, but will grow in understanding of the life of migrant ranchhands in the 1930s and in compassion for their hardships.

Words in themselves are neutral; they neither hurt nor harm. Their power comes from the context and the speakers' and listeners' reactions. As Hugh Rawson wrote in *Wicked Words* (1989), "There is nothing inherently pejorative about most of them and even the worst ones can be used in a nonthreatening way" (p. 3), which is the case in *Of Mice and Men. God damn it* is not blasphemy, but an expression of disgust, anger, or irritation. *Bastard,* once heavily tabooed, said Rawson, became "such a tame term in the 1960s that even a very proper paper like *The New York Times* would print it" (p. 3).

The way a word is spoken is very important. "Wicked words" can be intended to insult another or merely to show frustration or even affection (Rawson, p. 3). *Bastard* is sometimes used as a judgment about another's mean actions, but when George calls Lennie "a crazy bastard," he is neither talking about his parentage nor trying to offend. It is just a habit of speech, common to drifters, and Lennie loves the attention.

The community in Cookeville, Tennessee, it should be noted, was outraged not by the use of the book, but by its removal. Said the school board chairman, "Even my mother got onto me about the removal of the book. She told me we needed to get that book back into the classroom" (*Attacks on*, 1995, p. 28).

ISSUES: TREATMENT OF THE MENTALLY CHALLENGED AND OF HOMOSEXUALITY

THE CENSORS' CLAIM: George's behavior toward the slow-witted Lennie is rude and mean and sets a bad example for students on how to treat a person with disabilities. Because George has no obligation to take care of the younger man, he may be abusing him for sexual pleasure.

Controversial Segments

George says he used to play jokes on his simple-minded friend because he was so dumb, but Lennie didn't even know he was the butt of the joke. "I had fun," said George, "Made me seem Goddamn smart alongside of him" (p. 175). To show off in front of others, he once told Lennie to jump into the Sacramento River. Lennie jumped, even though he couldn't swim a stroke, and almost drowned. When they pulled him out Lennie was "so damn nice to me for pullin' him out. Clean forgot I told him to jump in" (p. 176).

The two men have come to a new ranch looking for work. George tries to protect Lennie by explaining to Slim, "He ain't bright. Hell of a good worker, though. Hell of a nice fella, but he ain't bright. I've knew him for a long time" (p. 173) and "He ain't no cuckoo. He's dumb as hell, but he ain't crazy" (p. 175).

COUNTERARGUMENT: George gives to the childlike Lennie the kind of patience, understanding, and love especially needed by those most vulnerable.

Despite the heavy burden, George keeps his promise to Lennie's aunt and looks after the younger, sometimes violent man who has no one else. George does get exasperated sometimes, thinking of how nice it would be to live by himself. He could get a girl, live in a hotel, shoot pool. He could, in fact, leave Lennie at any time and have a much easier life. But he doesn't, even though the two cannot keep a job because of the younger man's unpredictable behavior. Every time Lennie gets into trouble, George bails him out—at risk to his own life and livelihood. "Comfort the feeble-minded. . . support the weak," says I Thessalonians 5:14–15. That is the essence of this very moral book.

Lennie fears abandonment more than anything. He knows instinctively that he could not survive alone, and George knows it too: "Somebody'd shoot you for a coyote if you was by yourself" (p. 163). After the incident at the river, when Lennie almost drowned as the result of a practical joke, George learned his lesson and never did anything like that again (p. 176).

Despite his occasional gruffness, George takes good care of his ward. In the opening scene he prevents Lennie from drinking too much water after their escape through the woods. He is patient and sympathetic. "Poor bastard," he says to himself while Lennie is getting sticks for a fire (p. 160). Over and over George explains things to Lennie, who has a bad memory and difficulty understanding. He carries the young man's work card so it won't get lost and coaches him on how to act when they ask for a job.

One time George throws away a dead mouse that Lennie, who loves to pet soft things, has been carrying around in his pocket. When Lennie starts to cry, George feels remorseful and says later, "I been mean, ain't I? . . . I want you to stay with me. Trouble with mice is you always kill 'em" (pp. 16 2–163). What George fears is that his companion, who does not realize his own strength, will inadvertently kill something worse than a mouse.

To comfort Lennie whenever he is distressed, George tells him over and over about how they will always have each other to care for. One day, he says, they will be able to have their own place with a cow, garden, pigs, and especially rabbits. That is the best part for Lennie, being able to tend the furry rabbits. The story of the farm comforts both of them, but it is not just an idle dream, for George actually knows a place they can have for $600 if they can stay in one job long enough to save the money.

Although George evidently plans to take care of Lennie for a lifetime, nowhere is there evidence that this is more than the kindness of a tender-hearted man who made a promise to an elderly woman and feels compassion for someone who cannot fend for himself. Even if the "implication" of homosexuality were true, not all religious people, including those of the Christian faith, agree that homosexuality is a sin, especially for those who truly love each other.

ISSUE: RACIAL PREJUDICE

THE CENSORS' CLAIM: The book is offensive to African-American men because of the use of *nigger* and the obsequious depiction of Crooks, the only Black person on the ranch.

Controversial Segments

The other ranchhands named the African American *Crooks* after a horse kicked him in the back and twisted his spine. He is barred from the bunkhouse because of his skin color, sleeps in the harness room in the barn, has no friends, and behaves submissively around White people. When Curly's young wife comes uninvited into his room, Crooks is angry and tells her to leave. She snaps, "Listen, Nigger. You know what I can do to you if you open your trap?...I could get you strung up on a tree so easy it ain't even funny" (p. 195). Crooks is instantly reduced to a nothing, says the author: "There was no personality, no ego—nothing to arouse either like or dislike. He said 'Yes, ma'am,' and his voice was toneless" (p. 195).

COUNTERARGUMENT: Steinbeck shows Crooks to be a man of intelligence and dignity, but one who wisely knows how to protect himself, especially around a White woman.

Born in California to the only Black family in the area, Crooks sometimes played with White children when growing up, but was never accepted by the adults as an equal. He is understandably wary of all Whites. Steinbeck calls him a "nice fella," a "proud, aloof man" who keeps his distance from the others (p. 188). Lennie goes into the harness room and tells Crooks about the farm they can now get because of the savings of the old man Candy. Crooks asks to join them and confides how lonely he feels: "A guy needs somebody—to be near him....A guy goes nuts if he ain't got nobody" (p. 191).

When Curley's wife shows up, Crooks becomes rightfully apprehensive. A Black man in a White-controlled world, pointed out Steinbeck, led not only a lonely, but a precarious existence, saved only by erasing his self and retreating into mindless obedience. In this scene, Steinbeck shows the inhumanity that prevailed at the time, when African Americans, although no longer enslaved, were still treated cruelly and had few rights. For a Black man to speak to a White woman at all was dangerous in those days, and to tell her to get out of his room was a capital offense. After she threatens him with lynching, Crooks retires "into the terrible protective dignity of the Negro" (p. 194), not to grovel, but to survive.

ISSUE: SLEAZY CHARACTERS AND BAD ROLE MODELS

THE CENSORS' CLAIM: Almost all the characters in this novel are worthless, scoundrels, murderers, or sexpots.

Controversial Segments

Without considering the context or motives, one could describe all the characters as losers. Lennie squeezes animals to death and murders a young woman, George shoots Lennie in the head and kills him, the old man Candy is as useless as his sick dog, the boss' son Curley is violent with his wife as well as with the ranch employees, and Curley's wife is a whining slut. Only the jerkline skinner Slim and the Black man Crooks are halfway respectable, and in the end Slim approves of the murder of Lennie by George and believes it was necessary.

COUNTERARGUMENT: Each of the characters, except Curley whom all despise, is a likable, redeemable person when known to the reader.

Steinbeck once stated in a letter to his publishers that his books were aimed at "making people understand each other" (cited in Jackson, 1953, p. viii). He wanted them to see the good qualities in folks they might never meet in real life (or would reject if they did), to empathize with their traumas, to recognize that everyone has faults and failures, and to see the power of friendship and forgiveness.

For instance, Candy, who was a hard worker until his hand was mangled, knows he could be let go at any time. Like Lennie, he fears abandonment and having no one to help him in old age. When he hears about George's hoped-for place, he offers to put in all his savings if they will let him live there too. Candy's beloved old dog has outlived its usefulness, is sick and blind and smells bad. The other men think the animal should be put out of its misery. Candy cannot bring himself to do it, but at last agrees to let another man shoot the dog. Afterward, he lies miserably in his bunk, staring at the ceiling. George understands his grief and "binds up the brokenhearted" (Isaiah 61:1) by allowing Candy to join them in their plans for the farm.

Even Curley's wife is seen in death as having redeeming features. None of the ranchhands like her. George is disgusted with her flirtatious ways and Candy believes her own behavior caused her death. He blames her for destroying the dream of the farm: "You God damn tramp....Ever'body knowed you'd mess things up. You wasn't no good. You ain't no good now, you lousy tart" (p. 202). But Curley's wife, who has no name of her own, also has no life of her own. The only woman on the ranch, she has no companionship except her jealous husband who treats her badly. She is as lonely and frightened as Crooks and Candy, desperate for someone to talk to and to care for her. In despair, she goes to the barn just to find company. "I get awful lonely," she explains to Lennie in the barn. "You can talk to people, but I can't talk to nobody but Curley. Else he gets mad" (p. 198). She tells him of her dreams of being an actress. Her mother would not let her join a traveling show, so she married Curley to get away from home, then discovered too late that "he ain't a nice fella" (p. 199). She has come upon Lennie in the barn right after he accidentally killed a puppy. Seeing how bad he feels, she tries to console him. To communicate her understanding of his desire to pet furry things, she kindly takes his hand and lets him touch her soft hair. When he strokes too hard, she pulls away, frightened. He grabs tightly. She screams. He panics and puts his hand over her mouth and nose. She struggles. He shakes her angrily like other animals he has unwittingly killed and breaks her neck (p. 200).

Instead of the immoral *tart* the ranchhands think Curley's wife to be, Steinbeck depicts her sympathetically as a lonely young woman with crushed dreams, an abusive husband, and a dismal future. In death her youth and innocence is revealed, when "the meanness and the plannings and the discontent and the ache for attention were all gone from her face. She was very pretty and simple, and her face was sweet and young" (p. 201). Only the simpleton Lennie saw the tender nature of Curley's wife.

Each character in the novel is a unique individual who exhibits faults and frailties that help the reader see the complexity and heartbreaks of life and to develop empathy and concern for others. As the Bible says, "Who art thou that judgest another?" (James 4:12). Judgment of our fellow creatures is God's prerogative; our human duty is to "love one another" (John 13:34) and to "forgive, and ye shall be forgiven" (Luke 6:37).

ISSUE: RELIGIOUS INTERPRETATIONS: EUTHANASIA

THE CENSORS' CLAIM: Steinbeck reveals his anti-Christian beliefs in the description of Slim, whom he compares to a pagan temple dancer and to God. The final act, which he depicts as a "mercy-killing," is nothing but premeditated murder, which the "Godlike" Slim excuses as "necessary."

Controversial Segments

The jerkline skinner named Slim, says Steinbeck, was "the prince of the ranch," who "moved with a majesty achieved only by royalty and master craftsmen" (p. 172). He is just and righteous, with "calm, Godlike eyes" (p. 175):

> There was a gravity in his manner and a quiet so profound that all talk stopped when he spoke. His authority was so great that his word was taken on any subject, be it politics or love....His hatchet face was ageless. He might have been thirty-five or fifty. His ear heard more than was said to him, and his slow speech had overtones not of thought, but of understanding beyond thought. (pp. 172–173)

Slim's hands are as "delicate in their action as those of a temple dancer" (p. 173).

COUNTERARGUMENT: The description of Slim is not anti-Christian and the shooting of Lennie by George was indeed an act of mercy.

Slim is the one person on the ranch whom everyone trusts. His wisdom is great, his judgment final. He is intelligent, wise, kind, understanding, and patient—a person who exemplifies what God must have wanted when He made man "in His own image" (Gen. 1:27).

Like a loving Father, this humble ranchhand realizes that the shooting of Lennie by George was a merciful act, which saved the simpleton from a far worse death. Over and over, the concept of God as merciful and compassionate is emphasized in the Bible:

> "The Lord thy God is a merciful God" (Deut. 4:31)
> "His mercy is everlasting" (Ps. 100:5)

"The Lord is gracious, and full of compassion; slow to anger, and of great mercy" (Ps. 145:8)
"The Father of mercies, and the God of all comfort" (2 Cor. 1:3)

Central to the morality issue in this book is the "mercy-killing." Many people do regard euthanasia as a great sin, no matter what the circumstances. Others who are equally religious believe that, although taking a life is wrong most of the time, on very rare occasions when a situation is hopeless and the victim is in tremendous pain and soon to die, such an act mercifully gives comfort and release.

Concerned about saving Lennie from terror and violence, George ignores what might be the consequences for his own life. When he discovers the body of Curley's wife, he is sick at heart and knows that Lennie did not intend to kill her. At first he thinks he will tell the others and hope they will just lock Lennie up and not be cruel. But Candy convinces him that Curley will lynch the young man. Realizing that his simple-minded companion is slated to die, George decides to do what Candy wishes he had done with his dog—do the deed himself, and thus save Lennie from the torture of being hanged by others.

George finds his friend by the river, where he told him to go if he ever got into trouble. He has no heart to scold him for the murder of Curley's wife. He instructs Lennie to take off his hat and feel the nice breeze. He tells him to look across the river, while George gently, patiently recites the dream—the cows and land and rabbits and alfalfa. Lennie begs George to buy the farm: "Le's do it now." George answers, "Sure, right now. I gotta. We gotta." He raises the gun to the back of Lennie's head and shoots (p. 207).

The foreman Slim, humane and wise, the first to reach George, instantly assesses the situation and approves. He sits down beside the grieving man, offering support for a deed that has broken George's heart. "Never you mind," says Slim. "A guy got to sometimes. . . . You hadda, George. I swear you hadda" (p. 208).

Although Steinbeck's sympathies are clearly on the side of the shooting being an act of mercy, this is a moral issue on which intelligent, thinking people will disagree. Religious faiths (even those connected to Christianity) differ in their judgments about euthanasia, and individuals within those faiths also have opposing opinions. Reading and discussing this book will give students an opportunity to share their views, listen to others, and learn that moral dilemmas are often heartbreaking, involving a choice between two evils. No matter what one's religious convictions are, there are seldom simple, easy, ready-made answers to life's dire problems.

9

Religion and Morality in To Kill a Mockingbird *by Harper Lee*[1]

> "The one thing that doesn't abide by majority rule
> is a person's conscience"

Since its publication in 1960, Harper Lee's novel about racial bigotry in the deep South has been one of the most frequently selected books for required reading in high school classrooms. According to the Library of Congress' "Survey of Lifetime Reading Habits" (1991), *To Kill a Mockingbird* was second only to the Bible in being "most often cited as making a difference" in people's lives (Durst-Johnson, 1994, p. 14).

The book won a Pulitzer Prize in 1961, was translated into 10 languages, and was made into a classic film starring Gregory Peck as Atticus Finch. For 30 years, however, it has been on the list of the 30 most challenged books, usually in the top 10. Censorship attempts are made by those who claim racial bias as well as by the RR with their usual list of objections. In 1994–1995, *To Kill a Mockingbird* was attacked in Santa Cruz, California, because of the word *nigger* and "other derogatory names that reflect a negative portrayal of African Americans" (*Attacks on*, 1995, p. 61), and in Spokane, Washington, on the grounds that "the setting dehumanizes the African American child. It is belittling the African American student and race" (p. 223).

In previous decades, the book was temporarily banned in Eden Valley, Minnesota (in 1977), because of the words *damn* and *whore lady* and in Vernon-Verona-Sherrill, New York (in 1980) as a "filthy, trashy novel" (Doyle, 1994, p. 43). In 1981 in Warren, Indiana, the book was challenged because it "does psychological damage to the positive integration process" and "represents institutionalized racism under the guise of 'good litera-

---

[1]Page numbers for quotations are from the paperback edition, New York: Warner Books, 1982.

ture'" (Doyle, p. 43). In other states the book has been challenged because of profanity, racial slurs, and the word *nigger* (Doyle, p. 43).

Harper Lee wrote this novel, published in 1960, in the 1950s during a period of radical change.[2] In 1954 the U.S. Supreme Court ruled in *Brown v. Board of Education, Topeka, Kansas* that all public schools across the nation must be desegregated, causing a firestorm of violent protests in northern as well as southern states. In Alabama, Rosa Parks' refusal to sit in the back of the bus in 1955 and Autherine Lucy's attempt to enroll in the state university in 1956 helped augment the struggle to end legal segregation in the deep South.

Lee set her novel 20 years earlier, during the 1930s economic depression, when not only poverty but racial bigotry and fears were rampant. The trial of Tom Robinson echoes the infamous Scottsboro, Alabama, trial in 1931 when a White prostitute, afraid of being arrested on a morals charge, accused nine young African-American males, who happened to be riding on the same train, of rape. Despite the fact that two doctors reported no evidence of recent intercourse or any physical or psychological trauma, she was believed simply because she was White. All nine were convicted, eight received death sentences, and the ninth a life sentence because he was only 13 years old. Eventually, after numerous trials and many years in prison, with the support of civil rights groups and prominent individuals from the North and South, all were acquitted (Carter, 1969). In Lee's novel, however, the Black man Tom Robinson is not so "lucky."

During this time in the South, lynching was a common occurrence. More than 300 males, mostly Black, were hanged from trees between 1889 and 1940, often for trumped-up charges and without benefit of a trial. In 1930 this rose to about 20 a year, and others were shot to death (Durst-Johnson, 1994, pp. 5–6). No African Americans or women were permitted to serve on juries in those days, and professional men were routinely excused from duty. Thus, most trials were heard by poor, uneducated, White men who were often the most bigoted people in a community. In cases involving Black men, the jurors invariably ruled in favor of a White woman without regard to her reputation or the circumstances.

In 1934, almost 70 years after the Emancipation Proclamation, only four African Americans in the novel's setting, called Maycomb County, Alabama, are able to read and write. Women work alongside men in the cotton fields, either strapping their babies on their backs or leaving them lying in the shade between the rows of plants. As in the days of slavery, picking cotton for long hours is still their main occupation. They are paid poverty wages and have no education and little respect from much of the White population.

---

[2] See Claudia Durst-Johnson, *To Kill a Mockingbird: Threatening Boundaries* (1994), for an in-depth discussion of the background of this novel.

As noted before, some of the strongest objections to this novel come from those who believe it to be unfit reading for the descendants of Black slaves. However, it is also condemned by the RR because of language, the nontraditional Finch family, and interpretations of Christianity and the Bible.

ISSUE: RACIAL PREJUDICE

THE CENSORS' CLAIM: Being confronted with the problems of poverty-stricken Blacks in Alabama in the 1930s, and seeing the word *nigger* and other derogatory remarks undermines the self-esteem of African-American teenagers. The book condones the institutional racism that existed at the time—the segregated schools, housing, and courts—and is a depressing, humiliating, hopeless book.

Controversial Segments

Almost all the Black adults in Maycomb County are either laborers in the cotton fields or domestic workers in White people's homes. Only a few can read or write. After the imprisoned Black man Tom Robinson is shot trying to escape, White townsfolk said, "Typical of a nigger to cut and run...to have no plan, no thought for the future, just run blind first chance he saw" (p. 243). At Aunt Alexandra's tea party, after Tom is convicted, a woman fumes about the grieving unrest. She considers that unreasonable and childish: "I tell you there's nothing more distracting than a sulky darky....Just ruins your day to have one of 'em in your kitchen" (p. 234).

No Black children are permitted in the school that Scout and Jem Finch attend. African Americans live in "colored town" and must walk a long way to get to work. None are allowed on the jury, and those who come to the trial are forced to sit in the balcony. Although Atticus Finch defends the Black man Tom Robinson, he loses the case, as he knows he will from the beginning. The killing of Tom leaves a widow and fatherless children. And the segregated, bigoted, unjust life goes on as before in Maycomb County, Alabama.

COUNTERARGUMENT: The setting and events were indeed dehumanizing to the African Americans living in towns like Maycomb in 1935, and that is the point of the novel: to show the deep-seated prejudices and social customs that still prevailed into the 20th century.

As contemporary African-American writer Cornell West illustrated in *Race Matters* (1994), prejudice, injustice, and racial barriers still exist in America, not only in the South but across the country. Students of all backgrounds need to learn about our nation's sullied, bigoted past and present, and also read about courageous individuals, such as the fictional Atticus Finch, who put their lives on the line to protect the rights of citizens whom others in the community disdain because of skin color.

Far from debasing African Americans, this novel shows clearly how wrong segregation and racial biases are and elicits readers' sympathy for the plight of those forced to live in substandard environments on meager incomes and endure the acts of hatred committed against them. In contrast to the arrogance and disrespect of White people in Maycomb, those in the Black community are depicted as courteous, humble, and devout. The church is the center of their lives.

Despite its offensive connotation today, the word *nigger* was commonly used in the 1930s by White people everywhere in our nation, and thus is essential to this story in order to depict the reality of the times. In *To Kill A Mockingbird*, however, the Finch children learn from their father that saying this word is wrong. They receive lessons in civility as well as compassion and justice. For instance, after Scout gets into a fight with a boy who taunts her because her daddy defends *niggers*, she asks Atticus if this is true. He replies that of course he does, but she should not use that word.

"'s what everybody at school says."

"From now on it'll be everybody less one—"(p. 79).

Scout accepts that using the word is wrong and is thus confused when she and Jem go to a Sunday service with their African American house-keeper, Calpurnia. Another Black woman approaches angrily and asks why she is bringing White children to a "nigger church" (p. 121). The linguist Hugh Rawson explained in *Wicked Words* (1989), "'Nigger' is a prime example of how a word's meaning depends on context. Among most educated white people today, this is a hateful term, rarely employed, yet among blacks, it continues to be used casually, often approvingly" (p. 268). In fact, he stated, the word *nigger*, which had been used for centuries, was not considered demeaning, even when used by White people, until the late 1930s (p. 269).

Perhaps nothing changed for most people in Maycomb after Tom Robin-son's trial and death, but readers' attitudes today are often altered by this story of racial injustice and great courage. "Let justice run down as waters, and righteousness as a mighty stream" proclaims the prophet Amos in the Old Testament (Amos 5:21–24), but justice was poorly served in this fictional Alabama town for African Americans. The one person willing to stand up for their rights is the White lawyer Atticus Finch, who agrees to defend the Black man falsely accused of raping a White woman. Although Atticus knows the man to be innocent, he also knows he will not win the case. He tells his children that in the courts, when a Black is involved against a White, the White person always wins no matter who is guilty. "The one place where a man ought to get a square deal is in the courtroom, be he any color of the rainbow, but people have a way of carrying their resentments right into a jury box" (p. 223).

Scout, upset by remarks she hears about her father being a "nigger lover," tells Atticus that all the White people think he is wrong to defend the accused. He answers patiently, "Scout, I couldn't go to church and worship God if I didn't try to help that man....Before I can live with other folks I've got to live with myself. The one thing that doesn't abide by majority rule is a person's conscience" (p. 109).

After the jury finds Tom Robinson guilty, tears flood Jem's eyes. His father agrees that the verdict was unjust: "They've done it before...and they'll do it again and when they do it...seems only children weep" (p. 215).

ISSUES: FAMILY VALUES, SEX, AND LANGUAGE

THE CENSORS' CLAIM: None of the people featured in the novel live in a traditional family unit, the young people attend the rape trial where they are exposed to words and sexual acts they should not even know about at their age, and there are profane and blasphemous words used by the characters in this book, even the young girl.

Controversial Segments

The neighborhood in which the main characters live is indeed an assortment of non-traditional families. Calpurnia, the Black housekeeper, is the surrogate mother in the Finch family. Several women live alone, and Scout and Jem's friend Dill comes every summer to stay with his aunt to get away from his mother and stepfather who, he feels, do not want him around. The Radley brothers are recluses who frighten the rest of the townsfolk.

The Finch children call their father by his first name, Atticus, and talk to him as an equal. They continually question his actions and motives in defending the Black man. The young daughter Scout says early in the story that she is disappointed in her father because he does not drive a truck or work on a farm or in a garage, or do anything that is admirable. All he does, she says, is sit in the living room and read. Scout is even harder on Aunt Alexandra, who believes the children are undisciplined and comes to help raise them and teach them properly.

Scout, Jem, and their friend Dill disobey Atticus' instruction to leave the elusive Radleys alone. They try to peek in the windows, cover up how Jem lost his pants on the fence, and make up stories about these strange neighbors. On the night Atticus goes to stand guard outside the jailhouse, the children sneak out of the house late at night to find him, defy his order to go home, and almost get themselves killed by the mob.

Bob Ewell, father of the White girl who accuses Tom Robinson of rape, declares at the trial that he saw "that black nigger yonder ruttin' on my [daughter] Mayella" (p. 175). Tom states in return that he heard Ewell calling her a "goddamn whore" (p. 197). When Scout's older brother Jem tells her that she could get along much better with their Aunt Alexandra if she took up sewing or something else ladylike, she replies, "Hell no" (p. 228).

Scout's favorite relative, Uncle Jack who is a doctor, scolds her for using *damn* and *hell* in front of him (p. 84). Atticus, however, finds her outbursts merely amusing and ignores them. "Bad language," he says to his brother, "is a stage all children go through, and it dies with time when they learn they're not attracting attention with it" (p. 92).

COUNTERARGUMENT: The book is replete with examples of family values, such as love, patience, and respect. The rape trial is essential to show the cruelty of this Southern White community toward Black men, and compared to the derogatory phrases the townsfolk use toward African Americans, the bad words Scout sometimes says are very mild.

The children learn high moral values from both Atticus and their African-American housekeeper. Scout and Jem adore their widowed father, who returns their love and devotion. He reads to them, talks to them, and demands that they be responsible and courteous toward others, even those whom they fear or dislike.

Jem tells his sister, when she urges him to do something he knows would displease his father, that Atticus had never whipped him and he wants to keep it that way. Later, the feisty little girl, who normally attacks with her fists anyone who aggravates her, refuses to fight a boy who calls her father a disgrace for defending a *nigger* because Atticus had told her to ignore such taunts. It was hard to stay calm, but "Atticus so rarely asked Jem and me to do something for him, I could take being called a coward for him" (p. 81).

Scout began reading long before starting school, sitting on her father's lap and "wallowing illicitly in the daily papers" for years (p. 22). She is scolded for this by her first-grade teacher, who believes reading should be learned only in school. To the little girl's dismay, Atticus initially agrees to stop their reading together, realizing that the inexperienced young teacher is worried about succeeding and will make mistakes that need to be forgiven. Thus, he teaches his daughter about understanding others by putting oneself in their shoes.

Later, Scout remembers her father's advice that it is courteous to talk to people about what *they* are interested in, not what *you* are. When she, Jem, and Atticus are facing a threatening mob in front of the jail where Tom is held, she spots the poor but proud father of a classmate and politely asks about his son. Shamefacedly, the man tells the men to go home; her respect stops the violence and perhaps saves the Finches' lives.

The children secretly enter the courthouse during the trial and sit in the balcony with the African Americans in order to see their father defend the accused and uphold the law. They learn a little about sex, but a great deal about the democratic principles of equality and justice, and the lack of them for minorities. The charge against Tom arose because he befriended a poverty-stricken White girl who was abused and beaten by her no-good father. On the stand, Tom makes the horrendous mistake of saying he did odd jobs for Mayella for no pay because he felt sorry for her. No matter how deplorable her situation, this was considered a capital offense. Tom Robinson was not convicted because the jury believed he had raped a White girl, but because he had dared to say he felt pity for her.

The only lascivious wording in the book is the lie told at the trial by Bob Ewell about his daughter, who had lured the Black man into the house and then tried to kiss him. Her father knows that the charge of rape is untrue, but that is what will sway a White jury. The townspeople despise the shiftless Ewell, but the belief that a Black man might even look at a Southern White woman lustfully was enough in those times for a death sentence. Truth was irrelevant.

Scout blurts out bad words only when she feels controlled or abused or wants to disturb an adult. She is not trying to be profane or blasphemous. The girl reacts negatively to Jem's brotherly advice because she does not intend to compromise her freedom or her sense of self in order to please her insufferable aunt. She is rightly skeptical about Uncle Jack's telling her that his cat is getting fat from eating leftover fingers and ears from the hospital and says that it is a "damn story" (p. 83). As Atticus predicts, his daughter soon tires of the attempt to shock others and gives it up.

More important for the reader, Scout points out the hypocrisy of adults who condemn "blasphemous" words, but use ones far more hurtful and degrading to those of a different class or color. In addition to being upset over the word *nigger*, she is furious with her aunt who calls one of her classmates who comes from a poor but proud and respectable family "trash," and forbids her to play with him (p. 227). The little girl finds this especially onerous because it was Walter's father who saved the family from potential violence in front of the jail. She tells Jem that the boy is very smart and nice, but has missed a lot of school because he has to help his father provide for the family (pp. 227, 230). Unlike her aunt, Scout has learned to see and respect the inner essence of people rather than judge them on the basis of appearance and stereotypes.

ISSUE: RELIGIOUS INTERPRETATIONS

THE CENSORS' CLAIM: The book is antireligious, antibiblical, and immoral. It contains aspects of the supernatural, ridicules Bible-believing Christians, and contains a cover-up for a murder by the sheriff and lawyer unwilling to tell the truth.

Controversial Segments

Although the Finches go to church on Sunday, Atticus prefers to sit by himself. He evidently never discusses religion with the children or leads them in prayers. The Maycomb school has a costume party on Halloween, which the RR today considers an anti-Christian celebration promoting witchcraft. The children talk of "haints" and "Hot Steams" (ghosts), and Boo Radley is described as a "malevolent phantom." When the azaleas froze one cold night the townsfolk said it was because Boo had breathed on them (p. 13). When the children arrive home after Jem angrily cut the tops off a neighbor woman's camellia bushes, their housekeeper Calpurnia "by some voo-doo system" already knew all about it (p. 107).

Nathan Radley, Boo's father, is a "foot-washing Baptist" (p. 49) who locked up his son for 15 years after a boyish prank. The sardonic Miss Maudie, who lives across the street from the Finches, is also a Baptist, but says that her "shell's not that hard." She believes in footwashing only at home in the bathtub (p. 49).

One of Jem's favorite books is called *The Gray Ghost*, about some boys who chase another one thinking he is responsible for doing bad things. They run and run but can't catch him because they don't know what he looks like. According to RR believers, ghost stories are anti-Christian and part of the occult religion that is so dangerous to young minds and souls.

COUNTERARGUMENT: Religion per se is mentioned only occasionally in the book, mostly by Calpurnia and Miss Maudie, but biblical values are stressed throughout. Among the strongest are courage, justice, acceptance of others, and compassion.

Scout and Jem go with their housekeeper to the First Purchase African M. E. Church, named because it was paid for from the first earnings of freed slaves. Scout was impressed that everyone at that church dressed in their finest on Sundays to show respect for God. Although one Black woman objects to Calpurnia's bringing White children to visit, the rest of the congregation and the minister welcome them warmly. Said the always sensible housekeeper, "It's the same God, ain't it?" (p. 121).

Miss Maudie is outspoken in her criticism of hard-shelled religionists in the White community, and for good reason. She says of Boo's father, Nathan

Radley, that some men are so busy worrying about the next world that they don't know how to live in this one (p. 50). Maudie also loves nature, and her yard is ablaze with brightly colored flowers. A wagonload of stern-faced folk go past her home and call out disapprovingly, "He that cometh in vanity departeth in darkness!" She yells back, "A merry heart maketh a cheerful countenance!" (p. 161).

Maudie explains to Scout why she rejects such a negative interpretation of Christianity: "Foot-washers believe anything that's pleasure is a sin" (p. 49). She says that one Saturday some of them drove by her place and told her that her flowers were going to hell. "They thought I spent too much time in God's outdoors and not enough time inside the house reading the Bible" (p. 49).

Maudie, on the other hand, believes reading the Bible this way is not only foolish but dangerous. She says to her young neighbor, "Sometimes the Bible in the hand of one man is worse than a whiskey bottle in the hand of—oh, of your father" (p. 49). She means that Atticus, who seldom drinks, would know how to use liquor with caution and respect for its power, rather than overuse it and hurt either himself or others. Bible readers, she thinks, should approach the Scriptures in the same way.

When Aunt Alexandra bemoans how the townspeople, who normally respect Atticus, desert him after he accepts the responsibility of being the defendant's lawyer, Miss Maudie sees it differently. Whether they know it or not, she says, they are paying the highest tribute they can: They trust him to do the right thing. To the children she says, "We're so rarely called on to be Christians, but when we are, we've got men like Atticus to go for us" (p. 218).

Courage and determination in the face of defeat is one of the strongest values in the novel as well as the Bible. "Be of good courage, and He shall strengthen your heart," says the Psalmist (31:24, 27:14), and Ezekiel adds, "Be not afraid of them, neither be afraid of their words" (2:6). Not only does Atticus Finch stand up for an African American and withstand the ugly words and deeds from fellow White residents, he also displays bravery in facing a rabid dog that endangers the lives of the neighborhood. The children did not know their father could even shoot a gun, let alone kill with one shot, for he had not hunted since his early days and disapproved of killing animals unless necessary. When they are given air rifles by their uncle, Atticus tells them to shoot at tin cans, or at most blue jays—but never at a mockingbird for that would be a sin. Their neighbor Miss Maudie explains, "Mockingbirds don't do one thing but make music for us to enjoy. They don't eat up people's gardens, don't nest in corncribs, they don't do one thing but sing their hearts out for us. That's why it's a sin to kill a mockingbird" (p. 94).

An old and very ill neighbor, Mrs. Dubose, whom the children despise for her vicious tongue, is determined to break a morphine addiction before she dies. During her withdrawal attacks, she yells obscenities and other hateful words at the children as they pass by. In payment for destroying her flowers, Jem is ordered by Atticus to go read to the woman each day to find out "what real courage is, instead of getting the idea that courage is a man with a gun in his hand. It's when you know you're licked before you begin but you begin anyway and see it through no matter what" (p. 116). Atticus calls Mrs. Dubose "the bravest person I ever knew" and a "great lady" (p. 116). The children are incredulous, but learn that the abusive words are her way of coping with the intense pain during the period of morphine withdrawal.

Defending Tom Robinson is the ultimate in courage in a town dominated by White racists. Atticus places his reputation, his own life, and even his children's in jeopardy, though he knows there is little chance of winning the case. Why does he do this? "Simply because we were licked a hundred years before we started is no reason for us not to try to win" (p. 80). Like Mrs. Dubose, he undertakes the challenge despite the odds and sees it through no matter what the outcome.

Throughout the Bible, passages exhort us to love not only our neighbors as ourselves but also strangers, and to help those in need whoever they are. These virtues are exhibited repeatedly in *To Kill a Mockingbird*. Besides demonstrating care and respect for the African Americans in Maycomb, Atticus teaches his children about compassion for people who are different in other ways. Framing the book is the story of Arthur (Boo) Radley, the recluse who lives in a neighboring house. After his tyrannical father died—"the meanest man ever God blew breath into," said Calpurnia (p. 16)—the older brother took over and continued to keep the now middle-aged Boo confined.

The children have never seen the "phantom" and are both frightened and intrigued by him. Long after the trial is over and Tom Robinson has been killed, Scout and Jem are coming home on a pitch-black night from a school performance. They are attacked by Bob Ewell, the Black man's slovenly accuser, who still bears a grudge against Atticus. The children try to run, but Scout gets tangled in her chicken-wire costume. Jem is thrown to the ground, his arm badly broken, and Scout has her breath squeezed out. Suddenly someone else appears, kills the attacker with a knife, and carries the unconscious boy to the Finches' house.

Atticus believes it is Jem who knifed the attacker and argues against the sheriff's pretending the man fell on his own weapon. But when told that Boo Radley saved the children by killing Ewell, and that the townspeople would overwhelm him with their gratitude, Atticus' compassion overrules his legal conscience. Scout associates this with what her father said about their air rifles and understands: "It'd be sort of like shootin' a mockingbird, wouldn't it?" (p. 279).

After politely escorting Boo to his home, Scout finds Atticus sitting beside the sleeping Jem reading *The Gray Ghost*. She climbs into his lap and drowsily relates the story about the mystery lad who supposedly has done many bad things but cannot be seen by the other boys. When they finally catch him, they discover he has not done any of the things of which he was accused. "Atticus," says Scout, "he was real nice." Her father replies, "Most people are, Scout, when you finally see them" (p. 284).

10

Religion and Morality in The Grapes of Wrath by John Steinbeck[1]

"It's need that makes all the trouble"

In 1940, John Steinbeck won the Pulitzer Prize for this story published the year before of the plight of destitute farm workers who left their homes in Oklahoma, Arkansas, and other states for an even grimmer life in what they had dreamed would be the *promised land* of California. From the time of its publication, the book was attacked and banned across the nation. In 1939 copies were burned by the St. Louis public library and barred from the Buffalo, New York, library because of *vulgar words*. It was also banned that year in Kansas City, Missouri, and Kern County, California, where the novel was set (Doyle, 1994, p. 61).

In the 1980s, *The Grapes of Wrath* was challenged in schools in Iowa, upstate New York, Vermont, Alabama, and North Carolina (Doyle, 1994, p. 61). In 1990 a mural painted by elementary school children in San Diego, which included *The Grapes of Wrath* among other banned books, was ordered painted over by school officials (Foerstel, 1994, p. 196). In 1991 a parent in Greenville County, South Carolina, objected to this book and a number of others and obtained 2,000 signatures on a petition to have the works removed from the high school reading list. With the support of the majority of parents, plus teachers and students, the books were retained (Foerstel, pp. 196-197). Other recent demands for *Grapes'* removal have been in Greenville, South Carolina (1991), Midland, Michigan (1992), and Union City, Tennessee (1993; Doyle, 1994, p. 61; Foerstel, 1994, p. 197).

Besides the usual objections to profanity, vulgarity, sexual references, and using God's name in vain, the book is charged with humiliating Oklahomans, containing *collectivist propaganda*, and promoting an anti-Christian theology.

---

[1]The pages for quotations are from the Bantam Book paperback edition, New York: Viking, 1969.

In the 1930s, after years of cotton planting in Oklahoma, Arkansas, Kansas, and Texas on acreage better used for grazing, the land wore out. Crops were never rotated, winds blew away the topsoil, and production fell drastically. Owners replaced tenant farmers with tractors to save time and remain competitive, but continued to plant cotton until the land rebelled. Banks foreclosed on delinquent mortgages, forcing thousands of homeless families to surge westward in hopes of a better life.

"Pea Pickers Wanted in California. Good Wages All Season. 800 Pickers Wanted." Lured by the handbills that promised jobs and high earnings, tenants sold what they could for a pittance, piled necessities into a beaten-down truck, if they were lucky enough to have one, and set off with their hungry, ragged families to an uncertain future. Only a fraction of those who went West were needed for the fruit and vegetable season, but millions of enticing handbills were distributed, for the more workers there were who were desperate for jobs, the more wages could be slashed. Steinbeck's novel depicts in graphic detail what happened during this time to the working poor and the starving unemployed.

ISSUE: PREJUDICE AGAINST "OKIES"

THE CENSORS' CLAIM: Steinbeck humiliates Oklahomans by characterizing them as dirty scum—a legacy that, though very unfair, has persisted in many people's minds.[2]

Controversial Segments

Said one migrant in Steinbeck's story:

> Okie use' ta mean you was from Oklahoma. Now it means you're a dirty son-of-a-bitch. Okie means you're scum (p. 225)....Them goddamn Okies got no sense and no feeling. They ain't human. A human being wouldn't live like they do. A human being couldn't stand it to be so dirty and miserable. They ain't a hell of a lot better than gorillas. (p. 243)

In other sections, Steinbeck paraphrases the remarks made by Californians about the migrants from Oklahoma. They were called ignorant, degenerate, sexual maniacs, thieves, and disease-carriers whose children should not be allowed in the schools. "How'd you like to have your sister go out with one of 'em?" (p. 312).

---

[2]After the tragic bombing of the Alfred P. Murrah Building in Oklahoma City, April 19, 1995, when the nation saw on television the cooperation, compassion, and courage exhibited by those who rushed to help, the view of Oklahomans changed almost overnight.

COUNTERARGUMENT: Although these statements are hurtful to those from Oklahoma, Steinbeck throughout the book does not denigrate *Okies* but praises their humanity and survival spirit. He lambastes the unscrupulous landowners who lured desperate people West, then took advantage of them.

Born in the middle of the Depression, I lived in Oklahoma my first 24 years, but never read *The Grapes of Wrath*. No books were forbidden in our house, but the tone of disgust and anger my relatives used for the novel kept me from touching it. When years later I bought a paperback copy at a yard sale, I felt guilt and trepidation as I sat down to read. This soon turned to puzzlement. Why was my family so rankled? I doubt now that they ever read the book. Like so many who disapprove of literature, their judgment was probably based on a few phrases picked out of context and mistakenly assumed to represent the whole.

The story is not an attack on Okies, but on those who used and abused them. Frightened by the hordes of hungry people, said Steinbeck, Californians joined forces to defend their property. They armed themselves with clubs, gas, and guns and drilled at night for their vigilante work. The money that might have gone for wages went for agents and spies, for ammunition, for blacklists. Unwilling to help those they had seduced by their handbills, these "God-fearing" folk turned on the Okies and declared them subhuman.

Instead of the home the migrants hoped to find, wrote Steinbeck, they found hatred. The farm owners hated them because they were hungry but strong, the storekeepers because they had no money to spend, the bankers because there was nothing to gain from them, and the other workers because in their need to feed their families the Okies took jobs at any price and brought down the wages for everyone.

The author illustrates the inhumane tactics those with means used against those who were poor, who were struggling merely to survive. He does not demean the migrants, but condemns those who failed to follow the Bible's commandment to clothe the naked, feed the hungry, and help the indigent (Matthew 25:31–46). Although they called themselves Christians, they ignored such biblical statements as "oppress not the poor" or "the stranger" (Zechariah 7:9–10) and "he that hath two coats, let him give to him that hath none" (Luke 3:10–11).

Steinbeck admired the Okies' optimism, courage, and resilience and attacked those who oppressed them. The fictional Joad family, particularly Ma Joad, in caring for each other, helping others, pursuing with determination their goal for a better life, and maintaining dignity despite terrible times, epitomized for the author the best in humanity.

ISSUE: ECONOMICS

THE CENSORS' CLAIM: The book is a blatant attack on the free enterprise system that has given America the highest standard of living in the world. Collectivist unions are communist plots to destroy America's economy. "The free-enterprise system is clearly outlined in the Book of Proverbs in the Bible....Ownership of property is biblical. Competition in business is biblical" (Falwell, 1980, p. 13). If the poor worked hard and were responsible, they would be able to take care of themselves and their families.

COUNTERARGUMENT: The story illustrates the poverty and inhumanity that can result from laissez-faire economics gone amuck.

The novel is an indictment, not of the free enterprise system per se, but of uncontrolled power, social Darwinism, and those who call themselves Christian, yet hate, hurt, and degrade their fellow humans. Although Steinbeck used the 1930s dustbowl disaster for his setting and actions, the story's theme could be transplanted into other places and other eras, including our own.

Turned out by insensitive bankers at home, migrants soon faced Californians who lacked all understanding of how these families came to be in such despicable circumstances, and who felt no responsibility for luring them West or helping them survive. Nothing was done to relieve their misery. Forming unions and going on strike, despite the hardship on themselves and their families, was the only way the migrants could fight the landowners' stranglehold and gain any control over their lives.

Said Steinbeck, to the men desperate for work, true sin was in the fields that lay fallow, that did not produce, and therefore provided no jobs or food or shelter for the homeless families and their starving, thin children. Far from being *unbiblical*, *The Grapes of Wrath* exemplifies the main themes of the Bible: the call for justice, mercy, and compassion. The Bible is replete with commandments to help the poor, show mercy and kindness to those in need, and give just wages to workers: "The Lord will maintain the right of the poor" (Ps. 140:12); "Thou shalt open thine hand wide unto thy brother, to thy poor, and to thy needy, in the land" (Deut. 15:11); and "Woe to him...who makes his neighbor serve him for nothing and does not give him his wages" (Jer. 22:13).

Sharing and cooperation, rather than free enterprise and greedy individualism, are the concepts found in the New Testament. "Sell all that you have and give to the poor," states Luke 18:22. According to Acts: "There was not a needy person among them [for] distribution was made to each as any had needs" (Acts 4:34). In Israel, wrote Wayne Meeks, Professor of

Biblical Studies at Yale University, "there was a firm tradition, found not only in wisdom genres but also in the legal materials of the Torah and especially in the classical prophets, that God was especially the protector of the poor. God does not show favoritism toward the rich" (1986, p. 71). Jim Casy and Tom Joad's leadership in forming workers' unions was absolutely necessary to break the monopoly of the landowners, fight the oppression, and bring justice to the migrant poor.

The Okies lived as they did because they had no choice. *Filthy* was the term used most often against them, and being unclean bothered them greatly, especially the women. Although it had not been easy keeping the red dust out of houses and clothes back home, and wells frequently went dry in the summer, they had managed to stay reasonably clean. But on the road that was impossible. Lack of water forced them to accept smelly clothes, dirty bodies, and unsanitary food. What humiliated them most was the charge that they lived that way by choice and not from terrible circumstances over which they had no control.

The Joad family gloried for a few days in a government camp run by a humanistic director. Washing facilities, showers, and flush toilets were luxuries they had never experienced even at home. Not only were their needs met, they were treated with dignity and respect and could lead the clean, decent lives they were longing for. But lack of work forced them to leave and precipitated the decision that brought them disaster. The Okies were good people who worked hard, cared for each other, and shared their meager rations with anyone in need. Their plight was caused by the greed of those in power, not by laziness or the wrath of a vengeful God.

When a store clerk refuses Ma credit, but then gives her money out of his own pocket to buy something, she says quietly, "I'm learnin' one thing good. Learnin' it all a time, ever' day. If you're in trouble or hurt or need—go to poor people. They're the only ones that'll help—the only ones" (p. 415). Unlike those with means, the migrants loved their neighbors as themselves (Matthew 19:19) and found it "more blessed to give than receive" (Acts 20:35). According to Daniel Maguire (1982), the Bible is biased toward the poor. The burden is not on those who are poverty-stricken to explain their condition, but on the rich for permitting and profiting from it (p. 81).

ISSUE: FAMILY VALUES

THE CENSORS' CLAIM: Joad family members do not exhibit traditional American values and set a bad example for teenagers. Pa Joad is a wimp and Ma rules the roost, arguing with her husband, making demands—in direct violation of the biblical plan for the family—and the children are undisciplined and badly behaved.

Controversial Segments

Early in the book, when Tom invites ex-preacher Jim Casy to go with them to California, Pa is worried. They already have 12 people, a tent, mattresses, clothing, utensils, and food in one beat-up truck. Where will they put another person? Can they afford to feed him? Pa asks. Ma angrily retorts, "It ain't kin we? It's will we?...As far as 'kin,' we can't do nothin', not go to California or nothin'; but as far as 'will,' why we'll do what we will....One more ain't gonna hurt" (p. 111). Pa gives in without a fight and the preacher joins the group.

Family members are anything but perfect. Tom killed a man in self-defense in a fight and served time in prison. The oldest son Noah, who is somewhat slow and often in a world of his own, wanders off; Rose of Sharon's husband deserts her; and 10-year-old Ruthie is a contrary loudmouth. The elders are also quarrelsome and sinful. Uncle John admits that his alcoholism and inaction caused his pregnant wife's death. Grampa is lazy and Granma cantankerous. The Joads definitely do not fit the picture of the RR's ideal family.

COUNTERARGUMENT: Family togetherness, a very traditional value, is embraced by the Joads.

No matter what their members do, or what kind of personalities they have, the Joads love, care, and protect each other. Yes, Ma Joad is the mainstay, the strongest member of the family. Ma loves her husband, but both know that she is the sensible one. Her wisdom and moral strength are needed if the family is to survive. She loves each one and through crisis after crisis strives to keep them united, for no house divided against itself will stand (Mark 3:25; Matt. 12:35, Luke 11:17). Despite their elders' human faults, the children respect them.

When another family's car breaks down, Tom suggests the rest of the family pile into the overcrowded Joad truck and keep going West while he and the preacher go back to the last town to look for parts. He is sure they can catch up easily in a few days, but Ma stands firmly against that plan. She won't leave. "What we got lef' in the worl'? Nothin' but us. Nothin' but the folks....We got a long bitter road ahead....All we got is the family unbroke....I ain't scared while we're all here, all that's alive, but I ain't gonna see us bust up" (pp. 185-186).

Ma wins the first battle, but despite her efforts the family gradually falls apart. By the end of the story, Grampa and Granma have died and the nuclear family is in disarray. But Ma has now enlarged her definition of what it means to be a family by including others in need of care, comfort, and protection. The ties that bind humans together, she realizes, are made of more than blood or vows. As Jesus says, "All ye are brethren" (Matthew

23:8) and "Whosoever shall do the will of my Father, which is in heaven, the same is my brother, and sister, and mother" (Matt 12:50; Mark 3:35).

ISSUE: RELIGIOUS BELIEFS

THE CENSORS' CLAIM: The book is anti-Christian and blasphemous. The description of what the ex-preacher did at his revivals is horrifying, and the terrible ideas he spouts about religion will lead student readers into very dangerous thoughts.

Controversial Segments

The ex-preacher, Jim Casy, admits that he sexually abused some of the females who came to hear him preach. He "used to howl out the name of Jesus to glory" and "get an irrigation ditch so squirmin' full of repented sinners half of 'em like to drowned" (p. 20). When he runs into Tom Joad at the beginning of the novel, he says, "I used ta get the people jumpin' an' talkin' in tongues and glory-shoutin' till they just fell down an' passed out. An' some I'd baptize to bring 'em to. An' then—you know what I'd do? I'd take one of them girls out in the grass, an' I'd lay with her" (p. 22). Casy claims that sin is not something terrible but just a fact of life: "There ain't no sin and there ain't no virtue. There's just stuff people do" (p. 24).

He also says that he is not religious anymore, for being so means to him loud preaching, arrogance, hysterics, judging others. "Them people that's sure about ever'thing an' ain't got no sin—well, with that kind of a son-of-a-bitch, if I was God I'd kick their ass right outa heaven!" (p. 247).

COUNTERARGUMENT: The book presents religious ideas in keeping with the teachings of the New Testament and rejects the distorted, mean-spirited beliefs and behavior of the self-defined *Christians* in the book.

Casy claims that he does not know anybody by the name of Jesus, but throughout the story reveals Christlike behaviors. Besides having the same initials as Jesus Christ, he is a storyteller, loves people, forgives them their sins, and dies to save others.

Midway in Steinbeck's story, a Jehovah's Witness barges into the tent where Granma Joad lies dying and holds a noisy prayer meeting, singing and wailing. Later at the government camp another woman terrifies pregnant Rose of Sharon with a tale of two other girls she claims went to see the camp's stage plays and did "clutch-an'-hug" dancing and lost their babies because of these scandalous things (pp. 341–342). Casy rejects these "religious" behaviors and simply acts in a way far closer to Jesus' commandments to love one another, forgive them, and take care of their needs.

When Casy joins the Joad family, he is searching for a purpose in life. When he sees the misery around him—the men desperate for work, the starving children, the women who have nothing to cook each meal but fried dough made of flour and water—he finds his calling and a new meaning to religion. He tells Tom that every place he stopped, he found hungry folks who, even when they found food, did not feel fed. When they learned he was a preacher, they would ask him to pray for them. He used to do that, until he found that prayer did not make the troubles go away.

Tom interjects, "Prayer never brought in no side-meat." Casy agrees, "An Almighty God never raised no wages. These here folks want to live decent and bring up their kids decent (p. 275)....It's need that makes all the trouble" (p. 422).

Like Jesus, Casy rejected the view that religion is adherence to rules and doctrine. They both fought against those who oppress the poor and powerless. And both made the ultimate sacrifice—death for their beliefs and actions. Casy dies leading a strike for fair wages and decent treatment for the workers. "You fellas don' know what you're doin'," cries Casy (p. 426), reminiscent of Jesus' prayer, "Father, forgive them; for they know not what they do" (Luke 23:34). An assailant swings his pick handle. The club slams into the side of Casy's head, crunching the bone and killing him instantly. Outraged, Tom grabs the pick and strikes the man with a harsh blow. Dodging the others, Tom escapes downstream and into the brush.

Hiding in a culvert, Tom recites to his mother the Scriptural words (Eccl. 4:9–10) that Casy told him, "Two are better than one, because they have a good reward for their labor. For if they fall, the one will lif' up his fellow, but woe to him that is alone when he falleth, for he hath not another to help him up" (p. 462). These words convince Tom of the necessity of carrying out Casy's mission and uniting the oppressed who cannot better their lives alone.

ISSUE: LEWDNESS

THE CENSORS' CLAIM: The scene of Rose of Sharon in the barn letting a strange man suck her full breasts is a shocking, disgusting way to end the book.

Controversial Segments

Because flood waters surround the boxcar where the Joads are staying, what is left of the family—Ma and Pa, Rose of Sharon, and the two younger children—take refuge in a hillside barn. Inside they find a man and his young son. The father is starving because he has given what scraps of food he could find to the boy. Rose of Sharon, whose baby has just died, bares her gorged breasts and lets the man suck her milk, thus saving his life. The last words of the book read, "Her hand moved behind his head and supported it. Her fingers moved gently in his hair. She looked up and across the barn, and her lips came together and smiled mysteriously" (p. 502).

COUNTERARGUMENT: The scene is not lewd, but life-giving, and essential to Ma Joad's expanded idea of family.

It does not depict illicit sex, but lifegiving humaneness in a place where death and inhumanity are rampant. Despite their hardships, these Okies are the quintessential *pro-lifers*. Following Jesus' commandment to "love one another" (John 13:34), they do whatever is needed to survive and help others worn down by cruelty and natural circumstances.

Tom Joad recalls Casy's words: "Says one time he went out in the wilderness [like Jesus] to find his own soul, an' he foun' he didn' have no soul that was his'n. Says he foun' he jus' got a little piece of a great big soul" (p. 462). The Joad family, striving to live with self-respect and dignity, finds strength in cooperating, solace in caring, and sustenance in connecting to this larger soul of humankind.

11

Religion and Morality in I Know Why the Caged Bird Sings *by Maya Angelou*[1]

"In the struggle lies the joy"

This work by Maya Angelou, famed African-American dancer, singer, writer, poet, director, and civil rights activist, is the first in a four-book autobiography.[2] It recounts her childhood and adolescence, the divorce of her parents when she was 3, the move from one part of the country to another, from one relative to another, and ends at age 16 with the birth of an illegitimate son. It is not a pretty story. But it is a true one, told with humor, style, energy, and most of all compassion and understanding.

Those who object to the book find much in it that offends. The sex scenes and discussions are explicit, the characters are portrayed from the point of view of a painfully honest child, the behaviors and lifestyles of her parents and their assortment of oddball friends are relished rather than condemned, and the descriptions of religious people and services are hilariously irreverent or pathetically sad.

During the 1994–1995 school year, *I Know Why the Caged Bird Sings* was the third most challenged work in the nation (*Attacks on*, 1995, p. 11). In Hendersonville, Tennessee, the objection was to sexual references or situations. In Round Rock, Texas, with the assistance of Robert Simonds' organization, Citizens for Excellence in Education, critics attempted to have the book removed from classrooms on the basis of profanity and "encouraging premarital sex and homosexuality." Said one objector, an author's ethnicity "doesn't give them the right to titillate our kids whether they are red, black, brown, yellow, or white" (*Attacks on*, p. 24).

---

[1]The page numbers for quotations are from the New York: Random House edition, 1969.
[2]Followed by *Gather Together in My Name, Singin' and Swingin' and Gettin' Merry Like Christmas*, and *The Heart of a Woman*.

114

In Clovis, California, a parent argued for the removal of *Caged Bird* from an approved reading list for a Grade 11 and 12 elective American literature class because of its alleged "immorality, profanity and perversion" (*Attacks on*, p. 49); in Lake Tahoe, California, the book was taken off a Grade 9 summer reading list for honors English because of profanity and sex (*Attacks on*, p. 53); and in Memphis, Tennessee, the Christian Educators Association joined in the attempt to remove the book because they deemed it too realistic and the sexual scenes too explicit (*Attacks on*, p. 197).

Caged Bird was also challenged in Benning and Pleasanton, California; Bremerton, Washington; Haines City, Florida; and Hooks, Texas, because of the sexual molestation scenes (Doyle, 1994, p. 15). It was removed from a middle-school library in Southlake, Texas, because it contains "graphic profanities," is a "how-to book on how to live an immoral life," and "encourages pre-marital sex and lesbianism" (*Attacks on*, 1995, p. 205) and in Wimberley, Texas, because of its explicit sexuality and references to masturbation and rape (*Attacks on*, p. 207).

This autobiography of the growing-up years of a young Black female is about survival, hope, perseverance, and acceptance of self and others. For those students who live in poverty-stricken environments and nontraditional families or who have little control over their situations, the author is a real-life role model. By sheer determination she overcame low self-esteem, economic deprivation, and societal obstacles to reach the heights of artistic success and national acclaim for her civil rights leadership.

In adulthood, Angelou toured Europe and Africa as a dancer and singer in *Porgy and Bess*. She produced, directed, and starred in *Cabaret for Freedom*, wrote the screenplay and musical score of the film *Georgia, Georgia*, wrote and produced a 10-part TV series on African traditions in America, and wrote the TV screen plays for *I Know Why the Caged Bird Sings* and *The Sisters*. At the request of Dr. Martin Luther King, Jr., she was appointed the northern coordinator for the Southern Christian Leadership Conference. She has since received numerous honorary degrees and national awards. Angelou was invited by Bill Clinton to write a poem, which she entitled "On the Pulse of Morning," for his first presidential inauguration, January 1993.

Little in this book, however, foreshadows the later blossoming of the author's remarkable talent—only an eager mind (she read *The Tale of Two Cities* at age 8), strong will, and a budding interest in dance. Knowing about Angelou's troubled beginnings will appeal especially to adolescents in need of confidence and motivation. Privileged White students will learn how it feels to live as a Black female in a racially bigoted, male-dominated world.

In writing of her early years in Stamps, Arkansas, Angelou describes how both racism and economics oppressed the Black population. The primary occupation was cotton picking, which lasted only 3 months.

During that time, family members, male and female, had to earn enough to last for the entire year, but they never did. Their wages did not even get them out of debt to her Black grandmother, an enterprising, formidable woman who owned the general store, let alone allow them to pay the huge bills they owed at White people's establishments.

The Depression hit hard in the South like everywhere, but for several years African Americans barely noticed. "It seeped into the Black area slowly," she says, "like a thief with misgivings" (p. 49). With poverty already an everyday reality, there was little for Black workers to lose. Not until the payments to cotton pickers dropped from 10 cents a pound to 5, did they realize "that the Depression, at least, did not discriminate" (p. 49).

At age 3, the author, born Marguerite Johnson (and nicknamed Maya), and her brother Bailey, Jr., a year older, were sent alone by their recently divorced parents to live with their paternal grandmother in Stamps, Arkansas. Years later, Angelou learned that thousands of frightened, Black children traveled by themselves across the country to live with grandmothers in the South when the children's parents, who had gone North seeking jobs in the factories, were unable to find work.

ISSUE: WHITE RACISM

THE CENSORS' CLAIM: This is a racist book. It portrays African Americans as groveling, fatalistic field workers in the South or as immoral racketeers in the Midwest or West. The word *nigger* and other derogatory names are used, and Black leaders are shown to be wimps.

Controversial Segments

Maya's strong, quiet-spoken grandmother, Annie Henderson, was a businesswoman, the most respected person in her Black community, a woman of power and strength. Because there was no Black dentist in Stamps, when Maya woke one day with an excruciating toothache, her grandmother took her to the back door of the local White dentist who had borrowed money from her during the Depression. Maya cringed at hearing Mrs. Henderson announce herself to the young female assistant as Annie, as though she had no last name. This, Angelou writes, "was the heavy burden of Blackness" (p. 182).

The bigoted dentist refused to treat the child. When Mrs. Henderson reminded him of her generosity when he needed help, the man barked, "I'd rather stick my hand in a dog's mouth than in a nigger's" (p. 184). Maya and her grandmother were forced to take the 25-mile bus ride to Texarkana to receive treatment from a "colored" dentist.

At age 10, Maya was hired to work in a White woman's kitchen. Too lazy to say *Marguerite*, the employer insisted on calling her *Mary*. Not using Black people's names was a dangerous practice, Angelou notes, because of centuries of being called "niggers, jigs, dinges, blackbirds, crows, boots and spooks" (p. 106). The child got her revenge. She "accidentally" dropped several of the woman's prized family dishes and was immediately fired. That "clumsy little black nigger," screamed the distraught woman (p. 107).

Maya was an honor student in Arkansas, but the school she attended, Lafayette County Training School, unlike Central School for White children, had no lawn, hedges, tennis court, or ivy. It had two buildings and a staff with limited education. The girl stood proudly at her eighth-grade commencement, only to be humiliated by the White male speaker who read dully and condescendingly from his papers. He talked of the great improvements to be made in the science laboratories and art education at the White school, then praised the Black school for producing several good football and basketball players. In other words, the White children were being helped toward careers in science and the arts, whereas the Blacks were only expected, at most, to be athletes.

For the first time it struck Maya that no matter how intelligent, hard-working, talented, and ambitious African-American children were, in the eyes of White people, "we were maids and farmers, handymen and washerwomen, and anything higher that we aspired to was farcical and presumptuous. . . . The world didn't think we had minds, and they let us know it" (pp. 175–177).

On the other hand, Maya hated the apathetic attitude of Southern Blacks. The cotton pickers worked like oxen, Angelou writes, but pretended that things were not really so bad. She sometimes thought her people to be "a race of masochists." They lived the poorest, roughest of lives, then acted as though they liked it that way (p. 118).

The fight between Joe Louis, the Brown Bomber, and a White man for the World Championship fight was a critical point for Maya. If Louis lost, she believed, then the accusations made by White folks that Blacks were unintelligent and lazy and that God hated them and ordained them to be nothing but laborers forever would all be true. When Louis won, the Blacks huddled together for safety sake, fearing retribution from angry Whites.

COUNTERARGUMENT: Although Angelou disliked the kowtowing of Black people to Whites in the South and their acceptance of injustice, she understood the reasons. In this book she shows members of her race to be determined, resilient, strong, and resourceful, especially the women.

When the dentist refused to treat Maya's toothache, her grandmother used her ingenuity and wrested from him $10 "interest" on the money she had lent him, which paid the bus fare to the other town. As always, her grandmother stood her ground in a quiet, subtle way and maintained her dignity and self-esteem.

After the White man's insulting talk at the graduation ceremony, young Henry Reed gave his valedictory speech, then on his own initiative turned to his classmates and led them in singing James Weldon Johnson's stirring "Lift Ev'ry Voice and Sing," which has become the African-American national anthem. Instantly Maya's spirits soared, restoring her self-esteem and racial pride: "I was a proud member of the wonderful, beautiful Negro race" (p. 178).

Years later Angelou was enraged over the stereotyped picture of song-singing cotton pickers because she had seen in her youth the bodies of Black workers aching with fatigue, fingers bleeding from the prickly bolls. She realized that the resignation of the downtrodden Blacks was based on the belief that this was all they would ever have on earth, and thus they chose to be satisfied with their lot rather than be miserable over life's inequities.

In explaining the origins of her own strength, Angelou writes that young Black females are caught in the crossfire of male prejudice and White racism. "The fact that the adult American Negro female emerges a formidable character is often met with amazement, distaste, and even belligerence. It is seldom accepted as an inevitable outcome of the struggle won by survivors" (p. 265).

ISSUE: BLACK RACISM

THE CENSORS' CLAIM: This is a racist book by an African American who portrays all White people as arrogant, bigoted, hypocritical, and mean. It preaches bitterness and hatred against Whites.

Controversial Segments

In Southern states, African Americans were forced by law to use separate drinking fountains and restrooms and sit in the back of buses and in the balcony at movies. Atrocities against Blacks were frequent occurrences and Angelou gives numerous examples. For instance, when word got out that a Black man had "messed with" a White woman, the children helped their grandmother hide innocent, crippled Uncle Willie from the avenging Ku Klux Klan by putting him in a potato and onion bin and covering him "like a casserole." Most Black children in Stamps, says the author, had never seen a White person because of the total segregation, but they knew that such persons were to be dreaded. As a child she never even thought of them as people.

Fully aware of the dangers Black people faced in a segregated society, Mrs. Henderson taught her grandchildren not to risk their lives by talking to Whites, or even looking them in the eyes. They were never to speak about individual White people, but to refer to them only as *they*. The children's 10-year Southern stay ended abruptly when Bailey, Maya's 14-year-old brother, witnessed a dead Black man being fished out of a pond and White men laughing and joking about it. Their grandmother hurried them back to California to live with their mother. Said Angelou: "The Black woman in the South who raises sons, grandsons, and nephews had her heartstrings tied to a hanging noose" (p. 110).

Maya and Bailey experienced less overt but equally demeaning racism in California. The Blacks who moved from the South to the West to work in war plants soon found to their dismay that bigotry also thrived in California. The Southern Whites, who also moved there for economic reasons, brought their racial prejudices intact. For the first time Blacks and Whites worked side by side and "animosities festered and opened like boils on the face of the city" (p. 207).

COUNTERARGUMENT: Although Angelou gives evidence that many of the White people in her youth were bigoted, arrogant, and cruel, she also notes that they were caught up in a system not of their making. She does not preach either hatred or bitterness.

When Maya, at age 15, tried to break the segregation barrier against Black Americans becoming streetcar conductors in San Francisco, the incredulous White receptionist faked reasons for not letting her talk to the male manager. The two females, says Angelou, played out a centuries-old puppet play "concocted years before by stupid whites." However, instead of getting angry at the woman, the precocious Maya "accepted her as a fellow victim of the same puppeteer" (p. 260). Eventually, by determination (and faked statements of her own), Maya won the job and became the first African-American streetcar conductor in that city.

In her honest way, the author also points out instances of Black prejudice against other groups even more unfortunate and states the reasons. During World War II, the defense plants were in full swing in San Francisco. Many Blacks, including Maya's family, moved into an area left vacant by the interned Japanese Americans. One would expect, she writes, that the newly arrived Southern Blacks would sympathize with the Japanese, but they did not. Instead, they were blinded by steady paychecks and apartment houses, by taxis and restaurants. They were unwilling to share their new status with a race they never knew existed. Because the Japanese were not White, there was no reason to fear them or even consider their well-being.

ISSUE: VIEWS AND STORIES ABOUT RELIGION

THE CENSORS' CLAIM: The book is an assault on the Christian religion. The characters in the story who read the Bible, pray, and take religion seriously are ridiculed and criticized.

Controversial Segments

With rollicking humor, Angelou depicts the religion of her youth in the segregated region of Stamps, Arkansas: the obese Reverend Thomas who showed up at her grandmother's house on Sundays and ate the best parts of the chicken, Sister Monroe who turned church services into brawls, and Mr. Taylor's story about his dead wife's voice and a baby angel. The latter frightened the young Maya for, like most in her community, she was superstitious and believed in haunts, ghosts, and other supernatural beings.

Southern Blacks gave all the credit to God for whatever meager pleasures they enjoyed, Angelou notes, but did not blame Him for their many misfortunes. In childhood she admired a humorless taciturn man who never went to church. "How great it would be," she thought, "to grow up like that, to be able to stare religion down" (p. 20).

At revival-meeting times, the cotton pickers, instead of going home and resting their weary bodies, would gather to rejoice under the big tent, all the churches together. Some wondered, says Angelou, if the "Holy Rollers" with their raucous singing, dancing, and shouting would be allowed into heaven. At the age of 10, Maya worried whether God would permit his only Son to come into a revival tent to be with a lively crowd of poor Black farm laborers and domestic servants.

To her astonishment, Maya was whipped one day by her pious grandmother for beginning a sentence with *By the way*, meaning *incidentally*. Mrs. Henderson, however, considered it swearing because, according to the New Testament, Jesus was the Way, the Truth, and the Light. Thus, anyone who said *by the way* was really saying *by Jesus*, or *by God*, and the Lord's name would not be taken in vain in her house. These were White folks' words and an "abomination before Christ" (p. 100).

COUNTERARGUMENT: The author does not denigrate the Christian religion, but tells the stories she remembers about people and church services from her youth, her reactions and thoughts about religion as a child, and her adult understanding of the appeal of religion to poor Southern Blacks.

Raised by her grandmother from the age of 3 to 13, Maya went regularly to church meetings in the South and each morning heard her grandmother say a prayer upon rising from bed, thanking God for a new day and asking for guidance. Maya developed her own interpretations of Christianity. She thought her brother Bailey the greatest person in her world. The fact that she was his only sibling, "was such good fortune that it made me want to live a Christian life just to show God that I was grateful" (p. 21).

Deuteronomy was the girl's favorite book in the Bible because the rules were so absolute. All she had to do to avoid going to hell and "being roasted forever in the devil's fire" (p. 38) was memorize that book and follow it, word for word. On the morning of her graduation from eighth grade, before her high spirits were dashed by the White male speaker, Maya thanked God for being merciful about all the evil she had done in her life and for allowing her to experience this day. Somehow she had expected to die and never get the chance to receive her hard-earned diploma.

As mentioned before, one aspect that Angelou found difficult to accept was the fatalism that accompanied the religious belief of African Americans in the South. Although their history was harsh and their future insecure and threatening, they believed that only by God's mercy and intervention were they able to live at all. They thanked God for their meager subsistence and never blamed Him for their troubles. She adds drily, however, that as people become more affluent, they tend to attribute their good fortune less to God and more to themselves.

The Southern Blacks, writes the author, found in their religion a hope for a happy hereafter and revenge for their oppressors. Because God loved the poor and outcast, heaven was reserved for downtrodden Blacks and a few Whites like John Brown. Although White people had "their money and power and segregation and sarcasm and big houses and schools and lawns like carpets, and books....It was better to be meek and lowly, spat upon and abused for this little time than to spend eternity frying in the fires of hell" (pp. 127–128).

ISSUE: SEXUAL DESCRIPTIONS AND DISCUSSIONS

THE CENSORS' CLAIM: The book describes sexual activities, such as rape and intercourse, and promotes homosexuality, masturbation, and adultery.

Controversial Segments

When Maya was 8 years old, she lived with her divorced mother for a year in St. Louis, where she was sexually molested and then raped by her mother's lover. When she was 12 she served as a lookout for her brother's sexual adventures with a female classmate.

The author says that she read *The Well of Loneliness* as an adolescent, which introduced her to homosexuality. Although she was acquainted with gays and lesbians who came to her mother's house to cook and party, she did not consider them odd for "their laughter was real" and their lives were "cheerful comedies" (p. 266).

Like many teenagers, she was both curious about homosexuality and fearful that she herself might be a lesbian, especially given her physical characteristics. She was thin, almost 6 feet tall, had large feet, small breasts, and a very low voice. She felt awkward, unattractive, and unfeminine, and decided to broach the subject with her mother. Relieved that her daughter did not have "crabs" or a venereal disease, Maya's mother explained objectively that the "something growing" on the girl's vagina was called a *vulva* and was perfectly natural.

However, still worried, Maya decided that the only way to make certain she was not lesbian was to acquire a boyfriend and have sex. She set her sights on two handsome, popular brothers who lived nearby. When she met one accidentally on the street, she asked outright, "Would you like to have intercourse with me?" (p. 274). He was surprised, but agreed. A few weeks later she discovered that she was pregnant.

COUNTERARGUMENT: Angelou could not write her autobiography honestly without including the rape, sexual experience, pregnancy, and childbirth, all of which had lasting effects on her life.

The charges about promoting lesbianism and masturbation are false. Far from condoning homosexuality, Maya was terrified that she might be a lesbian. She accepted the gays and lesbians who came to her mother's house, but had no desire to join their circle. The girl's exploration of her changing body was normal for an adolescent. It was not done for sexual purposes but out of curiosity and an apprehension that something might be wrong.

Maya took full responsibility for the seduction of the neighbor boy. She had one quick unromantic, unenjoyable experience. Shortly after her high-school graduation, she delivered a healthy baby boy. She barely knew the baby's father, had no intention of marrying him, and was not upset when he stopped speaking to her. Although she regretted the experience and her own immature behavior that resulted in the pregnancy, this first book of the four-part series ends with her acceptance of motherhood and a joyful resolve to love and raise her child.

ISSUE: LANGUAGE

THE CENSORS' CLAIM: The book is full of profanity and blasphemy.

Controversial Segments

Early in the book when the exuberant Sister Monroe in Stamps, Arkansas, got into a physical tangle with the preacher during a Sunday service, the young delighted Bailey said out loud from the pew "Hot dog" and "Damn" and "she's going to beat his butt" (p. 42).

Although the children's mother cursed freely, according to Angelou, she did not allow them or anyone else to swear around her. When her restaurant–casino partner, who was not shouldering his part of the business responsibilities, called her a "bitch," the woman shot him—twice—although not fatally (p. 202).

After 15-year-old Maya and her father returned from a wild 2-day trip into the backways of Mexico, her father's new woman friend was furious. She called Maya's mother a "whore." Maya retaliated with "silly old bitch" (p. 239), slapped the woman, and ran away for a month of homelessness.

When the arguments between 16-year-old Bailey and his mother reached the crisis stage, the boy packed his bags in a fury and left home. He said to the grieving Maya: "Leave me the shit alone," "I'll be damned," and "To hell with her and everybody else" (p. 253). One reason for the crisis was Bailey's living for a while with a White prostitute.

COUNTERARGUMENT: Compared to books where the male protagonist is a boy, there are very few "dirty" words in this book.

In fact, what is recounted here is about the extent of it. Each of these incidents was in response to an especially emotional or traumatic event. For instance, young Bailey's reaction to Sister Monroe's outbursts in church is typical of little boys everywhere. He did, however, get a severe spanking from his Uncle Willie for his misbehavior.

Angelou remarks that her mother cursed frequently, but the words are not given in the book. The conversations of her parents' acquaintances, which no doubt contained much offensive language, are also not reported. As noted before, the author says that the children were never allowed to use profanity, either in their grandmother's house or in their mother's.

Sex-related words such as *vagina* and *vulva* were used objectively by Maya's mother to explain to her adolescent daughter the facts of growing up female—not to degrade or titillate, but to inform. The incident is used by the author to make the reader understand why she embarked on her plan to seduce a boy she hardly knew that resulted in the birth of her only child.

ISSUE: FAMILY AND VALUES

THE CENSORS' CLAIM: The book is an assault on the traditional family and American values. The children's parents, grandparents, and other adults live immoral lives, which are condoned rather than condemned, and Maya's childhood experiences are not ones to which impressionable teenage readers should be exposed.

Controversial Segments

Maya's paternal grandmother, who was married three times, owned a store and supported herself and her disabled son. Each of the girl's divorced parents had a series of live-in partners, which was neither uncommon nor reprehensible in their communities. Her uncles on her mother's side lived in St. Louis and were renowned for their meanness, beating up on Whites and Blacks alike "with the same abandon" (pp. 64–65). When the mother's boyfriend raped 8-year-old Maya and was set free because the child refused to testify against him, he was soon found dead. Maya had no doubt who killed him and felt responsible for his death.

In their maternal grandmother's home in St. Louis, during Prohibition days, the children met numbers runners, gamblers, lottery takers, and whiskey salesmen. They enjoyed going with their mother to a nearby tavern where she sang and danced. Later in San Francisco, Maya's stepfather, Daddy Clidell, introduced the girl to successful con men who taught her games so that she would never be "anybody's mark" (p. 214). Her mother played pinochle for money or ran poker games. She proudly used her quick mind in this way as a means of supporting herself and her children.

Maya did not regard any of her relatives or their friends as criminals or immoral people, but as individuals with intelligence and talents who made the most of difficult circumstances. Law violations, says Angelou, were looked upon differently in the African-American community of her youth. The feeling was, "We are the victims of the world's most comprehensive robbery. Life demands a balance. It's all right if we do a little robbing now" (pp. 218–219). The surprising thing, given the daily insults and oppression, was that more Blacks did not rob banks, embezzle funds, or engage in graft.

Blacks who lived in ghettos, notes the author, sometimes developed ethical behaviors that conflicted with middle-class mores. She gives examples of law violations and non-White middle-class behavior, but does not judge or apologize. She explains the phenomenon that Whites often find amusing—janitors or domestic maids who live in one room but buy flashy cars and expensive clothes. "In the Black American ghettos the hero is that man who is offered only the crumbs from his country's table but by ingenuity and courage is able to take for himself a Lucullan feast" (p. 218).

After running away from her father's place, Maya spent a month in a junkyard of abandoned vehicles, joining a commune of homeless children who scrabbled to exist. She did not go home to either parent, nor even call to let them know she was alive and all right. The adult Angelou praises the experience, claiming that it changed her life for the better.

COUNTERARGUMENT: Although Angelou's family may have been unusual, they were accepting, loving, and supportive people who could be counted on when help was needed.

Maya deeply respected her paternal grandmother in Stamps, Arkansas, who raised the children for 10 years despite economic hardship and the responsibility of caring for her crippled son. "I don't think," said the author, "she ever knew that a deep-brooding love hung over everything she touched" (p. 55).

When she was 13, Maya and her brother moved to San Francisco to live with their petite, energetic, fun-loving, beautiful mother who was a "hurricane in its perfect power" (p. 58). The two females were quite different in looks, temperament, and goals, yet the older woman doted on her tall, gangly, studious daughter, accepted her unconditionally, and encouraged her to go after her dreams. Although arguments between Bailey and his mother led to his moving out and living on his own, they loved each other and remained in contact. The children's dashing, irresponsible father was also important in their lives, and their stepfather provided stability and support.

The book contains many traditional American values that should be encouraged in students, such as the following:

1. Acceptance of Others. To her surprise, Maya was greeted the first morning in the junkyard by homeless children who had formed a commune with strict rules. No stealing (which might bring the police), everyone must work at something, and all money is community property. These children, Mexican-, African-, and Euro-American, initiated her into the "brotherhood of man" that "set a tone of tolerance" for her life (p. 247).

2. Acceptance of Self. As a child in Arkansas, Maya longed to be White, to have straight blonde hair and blue eyes instead of a "too-big Negro girl, with nappy black hair, broad feet and a space between her teeth that would hold a number-two pencil" (pp. 4–5). During her month-long experience in the junkyard, she gained confidence and self-esteem through the other children's unquestioning acceptance. For the first time she felt a part of the human race, rather than apart from it.

3. Love of Learning. When Maya returned to Arkansas after the rape in St. Louis, she refused to speak to anyone except her brother Bailey. Her wise grandmother introduced her to a woman, a Black aristocrat, who gave her books to read and urged her to memorize and recite poetry. Mrs. Flowers was "one of the few gentlewomen I have ever known, and has remained throughout my life the measure of what a human being can be." The woman "made me proud to be Negro, just by being herself" (p. 91).

4. Goal Setting and Determination. When Maya at 15 decided she wanted a job—and one that was denied to her race—her mother was her strongest supporter. She encouraged the girl to "give it everything you've got" (p. 258). Maya's mother was full of aphorisms, which she not only spouted but modeled. She taught her children to reject the hopeless, helpless, victim status, and follow their dreams and aspirations. Accept life as it is without

remorse, she urged, but also work for equality and a better society. The woman, wrote Angelou, "comprehended the perversity of life, that in the struggle lies the joy" (p. 261).

I Know Why the Caged Bird Sings is a positive contribution to biographical literature. This poetically written account of an adolescent, minority female experience is both convincing and moving. Angelou demonstrates the evils of sexism and racism as well as the importance of love, courage, and hope.

Reading this book, however, requires for most White middle-class students a suspension of learned beliefs in order to walk in the shoes of another person without judgment. If they can do that, they will gain valuable insight about the pains of oppression and the difficulty of growing up Black and female in a society dominated by Whites and males.*

---

*A shorter version of this chapter was published in 1985 as "'I know why the caged bird sings': Awareness of displacement." In N. J. Karolides & L. Burress (Eds.), *Celebrating the censored book!* (pp. 61–63). Racine, WI: Wisconsin Council of Teachers of English.

III

SUGGESTIONS FOR PREVENTING AND RESPONDING TO CHALLENGES

12

Suggestions for Preventing
and Responding to Challenges

The literary works discussed in this book are filled with the humor, drama, and pathos of human lives and demonstrate that moral issues are an integral part of living in this world. For many people, the choices that are made in their lives are based on religious convictions, either consciously or intuitively. In trying to understand the motives and actions of characters in novels as well as persons in real life, an exploration of their religious beliefs is a helpful and valid endeavor. Readers' reactions to these works will be highly influenced by their own religious outlook.

Most books worth reading will involve readers in moral dilemmas and engage them in issues saturated with religious implications. The American public school, with its religiously diverse clientele and its commitment to open discussion, is an excellent arena for airing a variety of beliefs, analyzing their impact on human behavior, and aiding students in the discovery of their own convictions.

The teacher's role is vital in helping students recognize the issues and dilemmas and in facilitating democratic, insightful discussions that are respectful of various ideas and those who express them. When handled well, students will exhibit growth in the development of their own beliefs about what is religious, what is moral, and in what ways literature can guide and enrich their lives.

However, individuals and organized groups in our country have challenged many books that have been selected for public school classrooms and libraries because of what they perceive to be immoral, antireligious, anti-Christian, or antibiblical content. Procedures must be developed by teachers, librarians, administrators, and school boards that are aimed at both preventing confrontations and responding to those that continue to arise. The following suggestions are given to help educators plan ahead for possible challenges to books, programs, or teaching strategies so they are well prepared for any eventuality.

What Can School Districts and Educators Do to Protect Themselves Against Attacks on Books or Teaching Methods?

- Have a textbook review committee in each school district, appointed by the school board, made up of teachers, administrators, and several parents who represent diverse community views.
- Have in place carefully designed policies for handling complaints about books and other teaching materials (see sample form in Appendix B).
- Have a committee for the reconsideration of materials, appointed by the school board, similar in makeup to the textbook review committee, but involving different personnel (see more on this following).
- Offer workshops for teachers on the need for book rationales, how to write them, and how to recognize and handle possible controversial issues.
- Put all rationales for assigned book selections in writing. These should be filed in the school office and made available on request by school personnel or parents.
- Have all selected books ready for parents to browse through at an open house early in the school year.
- Discuss openly any new programs or teaching methods, explaining the reasons and benefits, answering concerns and questions. Many objections arise out of misunderstandings, misconceptions, and rumors spread by people who have never read the books or seen the teaching techniques in action.
- Explain to parents and older students that they always have the right to an alternative book or assignment, if what is planned offends their beliefs or values. If you think a book may be a problem for some students or parents, have a list of alternatives to suggest.
- Invite parents to visit their children's classrooms so they can see for themselves how books are presented and activities conducted. Make them feel sincerely welcome at all times in the school.
- Actively seek out the involvement of all parents in constructive ways in the school, not just those who volunteer. Some parents had poor experiences in their own school days, are doubtful of their acceptance by other parents, and are intimidated by teachers, administrators, and the building itself. When parents have positive feelings about their children's school and feel their help is valued, they are more willing to work out amicable solutions to whatever concerns they may have.

What Should You Do When Parents Object
to Reading Material?

- Do not jump to the conclusion that they are members of one of the RR organizations discussed in this book and become defensive or adversarial. We do want parents to be concerned about their children and interested in what they are learning. Praise the parent for knowing what the child is reading and doing in school. Many do not know or do not care.
- Do not doubt the parents' sincerity. They may admit they have not read the book in question, or have read only portions taken out of context, but they are earnest in their belief that what they have seen or heard is offensive to their religious and moral values.
- Ask a colleague, especially one who has effectively resolved a similar complaint, to facilitate the discussion or at least be present as a witness.
- Listen carefully and courteously to the objection without comment. Ask why the parents feel a story or activity is wrong for children. Mirror back what is said so they know they have been heard and taken seriously.
- Explain why the book or activity was chosen, giving your reasons in a calm, objective manner. Be sure you have good reasons that you have thought through ahead of time. Having them in writing ensures that you have developed good rationales and enables you to refer to them at a time when your emotional state may interfere with your thoughts.
- Try to resolve the problem informally. Offer to give the child an acceptable alternate assignment or another activity in lieu of the one objected to. Usually that will satisfy the parent and a good relationship will have been developed, which is very important for the well-being of the child.

What If That Doesn't Work?

What if you are faced with a parent who is convinced that a book is evil or a teaching technique is damaging not only to his or her child but all children? Who is threatening to sue you, the school district, and everyone in sight? This can be frightening. Such a person is perhaps being coached by one of the national RR groups and does not plan to give in until the book or program is removed from the school. The challenger's goal is to intimidate the teacher, librarian, and administrator and undermine their professional authority.

- Stay cool and calm and state firmly but politely that a book or teaching strategy will not be changed or eliminated because of the request of one parent or even several. The other children in the classroom have a right to read books and be taught according the teacher's best professional judgment. Their parents have the same right as the critics to voice opinions about what is read in school.
- Inform the parent that the school district has a policy with regard to challenges, which you are required to follow—and do so, to the letter.
- Give the parent a formal complaint form, such as the one reproduced in Appendix B. Keep copies in your desk. In order to fill out the form, a parent must read the book or other materials and be specific about the objections. This also gives you time to report the challenge, review the district's policy, obtain advice from administrators, colleagues, and perhaps your union, and respond professionally.
- Refuse to discuss the matter any further with the complainant until the form has been completed and turned into the school office. If necessary, call in the principal or a colleague for support. Just because a parent has confronted you does not mean you have to talk at that particular time.
- Assure the parent that the matter will be given serious attention. The completed form should be turned over by your principal to the committee for reconsideration of materials.
- Unless forbidden by school administrators (see Homstad, *Anatomy of a Book Controversy*, 1995), continue to use the book in class until the committee has come to a decision. Explain to the students, without naming or criticizing the parent, that a complaint has been lodged.
- Protect the child of the parent making the complaint from negative remarks or harassment by other students during class time.
- Make no negative remarks in public, to your colleagues, or especially to the press about the objector. You can state your convictions about the positive aspects of the book without denouncing the complainant.

What If the Parent Persists?

At this point, the objection has gone beyond the classroom teacher and become a school problem, a district problem, a professional education problem. When the complaint concerns aspects that parents find offensive to their religious beliefs or moral values, an alternative for their own child will probably not suffice. A compromise is not acceptable. The purpose is to protect all children, even if the other parents believe the book is worthwhile.

- School administrators should inform the public of any written complaints, and the committee for reconsideration of materials should conduct an open review of the material under attack. This may invite more objections, but it will also bring out those who approve of the book or teaching method. They have the same right to speak *for* a book as those who speak against it. All parents ought to know what is being challenged, and why, and be given the opportunity to state their views.

- If the situation escalates, the best place for teachers, librarians, and school districts to turn are national education and anticensorship organizations. These groups have dealt with such problems many times before and have experts who will give advice and sometimes legal counsel and funds to help pay for court battles. The addresses of several of the most prominent are listed in Appendix C.

- Finally, if the committee for reconsideration of materials has followed the district's policy, has held open meetings, and has recommended eliminating a book from a reading list or limiting its availability, and this has been approved by the school board, the teacher involved probably has little choice but to accept the decision or lose his or her job. The school board does have the legal right and responsibility to oversee book selections.

Accepting the decision without rancor can, however, be an excellent lesson for students about democracy, cooperative living, and religious plurality. Not only do citizens in America, including children, have the right to read and discuss ideas, but they have the right to raise objections and try to change whatever they feel is morally wrong. And others, including teachers, have the right to defend what they believe is morally right.

Although one may lose the conflict over a particular book, the larger goal for public education is to confront students with a variety of ideas and accurate information, allow them some choices and the opportunity to voice opinions, teach them by precept and example to respect the rights of others, have a wide range of reading material readily available, and demonstrate the courage to stand up for what is intellectually challenging, culturally diverse, and democratically sound.

Appendix A

Sources for Preventing and Responding to Challenges

Attacks on the freedom to learn, 1994–1995 report. (1995; p. 34). Washington, DC: People for the American Way.

Bartlett, L. (1979). The Iowa model policy and rules for selection of instructional materials. In J. E. Davis (Ed.), *Dealing with censorship* (pp. 202–214). Urbana, IL: National Council of Teachers of English.

Bruwelheide, J. H. (1987). Reasons to fight censorship. *Clearing House, 60,* 416–417.

Censorship: A continuing problem. (1990). *English Journal, 79*(5), 87–89.

Censorship: Managing the controversy (1989). Alexandria, VA: National School Boards Association.

Daly, J. K. (1995). Building support for intellectual freedom. *Contemporary Education, 66,* 92–95.

Donelson, K. L. (1979). Censorship in the 1970's: Some ways to handle it when it comes (and it will). In J. E. Davis (Ed.), *Dealing with censorship* (pp. 162–167). Urbana, IL: National Council of Teachers of English.

Fege, A. F. (1990). Academic freedom and community involvement: maintaining the balance. In A. S. Ochoa (Ed.), *Academic freedom to teach and to learn: Every teacher's issue* (pp. 48–59). Washington, DC: National Education Association.

Fege, A. F. (1991). Censorship in the schools. *PTA Today, 16* (5), 10–12.

Harrington-Lueker, D. (1991). Book battles. *American School Board Journal, 178*(2) 18–21, 37.

Hopkins, D. M. (1993). Factors influencing the outcomes of challenges to materials in secondary schools. *School Library Media Annual, 11,* 167–168.

How to arm for battle with pressure groups (1992). *School Administrator 49* (4), pp. 14–16, 18.

Jenkinson, E. B. (1990). Lessons learned from three schoolbook protests. In A. S. Ochoa (Ed.), *Academic freedom to teach and to learn: Every teacher's issue* (pp. 60–76). Washington, DC: National Education Association.

Jenkinson, E. B. (1995). Myths and misunderstandings surround the schoolbook protest movement. *Contemporary Education, 66,* 70–73.

Jones, J. L. (1990). Countering far right tactics. In A. S. Ochoa (Ed.), *Academic freedom to teach and to learn: Every teacher's issue* (pp. 79–104). Washington, DC: National Education Association.

Jones, J. L. (1993). Targets of the right. *American School Board Journal 180*(4), 22–29.

McCarthy, M. (1993). Challenges to public school curriculum. *Phi Delta Kappan, 75,* 55–56, 58–60.

O'Neal, S. (1990). Controversial books in the classroom. *Language Arts, 67,* 771–775.

Reichman, H. (1988). *Censorship and selection: Issues and answers for schools.* Chicago, IL: American Library Association.

Shugert, D. P. (1979). How to write a rationale in defense of a book. In J. E. Davis. (Ed.), *Dealing with censorship* (187–201). Urbana, IL: National Council of Teachers of English.

Simmons, J. (1991). Censorship in schools: No end in sight. *ALAN Review, 18*(2), 6–8.

Stern, M. E. (1994). A plan of action for secondary English teachers. In J. E. Simmons (Ed.), *Censorship: A threat to reading, learning, thinking* (pp. 198–210). Newark, DE: International Reading Association.

Suhor, C. (1979). Basic training and combat duty—preventive and reactive action. In J. E. Davis (Ed.), *Dealing with censorship* (168–179). Urbana, IL: National Council of Teachers of English.

Appendix B

Sample *"Request for Reconsideration"**

Request for Reconsideration

Please complete this form and submit it to (designated administrator: _____
by (date): _____

Author: _____ Title: _____

Text: _____ Library book: _____ Magazine: _____ Film/video: _____ Other: _____

Publisher: _____ Publication Date: _____

Request initiated by: _____
Street Address: _____
City: _____ State: _____ZIP: _____ Phone:_____

Citizen represents:
_____ Self
_____ Organization (identify) _____
_____ Other group (identify) _____

1. To what in the book or material do you object? Please cite specific pages.
_____

2. Why do you object to the use of this material?
_____
_____
_____

3. Have you read or viewed the entire contents? _____ Yes _____ No

4. What pages or portions did you read or view? _____

5. What would you like your school to do about this material?
_____ Do not assign or recommend it to my child.
_____ Place on restricted use (parental approval required).
_____ Other: _____
Comments: _____
_____
_____

District Policy (number) _____ and related Procedures (number) _____ detail the pro-
cesses and timelines that will be followed upon receipt of this form by the above named
administrator. Copies of these policies and procedures are available upon request.

_____   _____ 19 _____
Signature   Date

For District Use: Date Received: _____ By Whom? _____

---

*Academic freedom to teach and learn: Every teacher's issue, Anna S. Ochoa, Ed. Appendix by Janet L. Jones. Copyright 1990. Washington, DC: National Education Association. Reprinted by permission of the NEA Professional Library.

Appendix C

Organizations Against Censorship

National Council of Teachers of English
1111 W. Kenyon Road
Urbana, IL 61801–1096
(217) 328-3870

People for the American Way
2000 M Street, NW
Suite 400
Washington, DC 20036
(202) 467-4999

Office for Intellectual Freedom
American Library Association
50 East Huron Street
Chicago, IL 60611
(800) 545-2433, Extension 4223

National Education Association
1201 16th Street, NW
Washington, DC 20036
(202) 833-4000

American Federation of Teachers
555 New Jersey Avenue, NW
Washington, DC 20001-2070
(800) 238-1133

National Coalition Against Censorship
275 Seventh Avenue, 20th Floor
New York, NY 10001
(212) 807-6222

References

Abington v. Schempp; Murray v. Curlett, 10 L.Ed.2d 844 (1963).

Adams, D. W. (Ed.). (1983). *Jefferson's extracts from the Bible.* Princeton, NJ: Princeton University Press.

The American cause, Pat Buchanan's new group comes up with ideas on how to win the culture war. (1996, May 25). Internet.

Angelou, M. (1969). *I know why the caged bird sings.* New York: Random House.

Architect of Christian Coalition's clout moves on (1997, April 24). *The Daily Star,* Oneonta, NY, p. 2.

Attacks on the freedom to learn. (1995). Washington, DC: People for the American Way.

The banning of Billy Pilgrim. (1971). *The Christian Century, 88,* 681.

Barton, D. (1992). *The myth of separation.* Aledo, TX: Wallbuilders Press.

Bednarek, D. I. (1986, August 10). Group's goal: To reshape schools. *The Milwaukee Journal,* p. B-3.

Bellah, R. N. (1974). Civil religion in America. In R. E. Richey & D. G. Jones (Eds.), *American civil religion* (pp. 21–44). New York: Harper & Row.

Bergstrom, C. (1985, November 11). The new faces of American bigotry. *The Oakland Tribune,* p. 4.

Bollier, D. (1984). The witch hunt against "secular humanists." *The Humanist, 40*(5), 11–19, 50.

Boorstin, D. (1992). *The creators: A history of heroes of the imagination.* New York: Random House.

Booth, W. C. (1988). *The company we keep: An ethics of fiction.* Berkley: University of California Press.

Boston, R. (1995). Uncivil religion. *Church and State 48*(9), 11–13.

Boston, R. (1996a). Consumer alert! Wallbuilders' shoddy workmanship. *Church and State 49*(7), 11–13.

Boston, R. (1996b). *The most dangerous man in America? Pat Robertson and the rise of the Christian Coalition.* Amherst, NY: Prometheus.

Boston, R. (1996c). Pat Robertson and church–state separation: A track record of deception. *Church and State 49*(4), 9–13.

Boston, R. (1997). God's will, Newt's agenda. *Church and State 56*(1), 4–7.

Bradley, A. (1995). Christian Coalition offers tips on promoting vouchers. *Education Week 15* (3), 7.

Brown v. Board of Education, Topeka, Kansas, 74 S. Ct. 686, 98 F. Supp. 797 (1954).

Bullough, V. L. (1996). Church and state: A humanist view. *Free Inquiry 16*(2), 9–11.

Calvino, I. (1986). *The uses of literature* (P. Creagh, Trans.). New York: Harcourt Brace Jovanovich. (Original work published 1980)

Cantor, D. (1994). *The religious right: The assault on tolerance and pluralism in America* (2nd ed.). New York: Anti-Defamation League.

Carter, D. (1969). *Scottsboro: A tragedy of the American South.* Baton Rouge: Louisiana State University Press.

Carter, J. (1996). *Living faith.* New York: Random House.

Cohen, D. L. (1996). Child care not seen hurting bond with mother. *Education Week 15*(32), 7.

Coles, R. (1989). *The call of stories: Teaching and the moral imagination.* Boston: Houghton Mifflin.

Conn, J. L. (1995). Power trip. *Church and State 48*(9), 4–7.

Conn, J. L. (1996a). Bad trip. *Church and State 49*(9), 4–7.

Conn, J. L. (1996b). Bully Pulpit. *Church and State 49*(5), 11–12.

Conn, J. L. (1996c). Mutiny on the right. *Church and State 49*(11), 4–6.

Conn, J. L. (1996d). Pyramid scheme. *Church and State 49*(3), 4–11.

Constitutional amendment follies: Refuting the religious right's big lie (1995). *Church and State 48*(10), 13.

Coontz, S. (1996). Where are the good old days? *Modern Maturity, 39* (3), 36–43.

Cormier, R. (1994). A book is not a house: The human side of censorship. In J. S. Simmons (Ed.), *Censorship: A threat to reading, learning, thinking* (pp. 62–72). Newark, DE: International Reading Association.

Court rules reading series does not violate rights. (1994). *Education Week 13*(21), 5.

Cunningham, N. E., Jr. (1987). *In pursuit of reason: The life of Thomas Jefferson.* Baton Rouge: Louisiana State University.

The debate: Whether and how to censor "objectionable" school books (1973). *American School Board Journal 160*(5), 39.

Dewey, J. (1939). *Freedom and culture.* New York: G. P. Putnam's Sons.

Doyle, R. P. (1994). *Banned books: 1994 resource guide.* Chicago: American Library Association.

Durst-Johnson, C. (1994). *To kill a mockingbird: Threatening boundaries.* New York: Twayne.

Edwards, J. K. (1977). *The obscenity issue in textbook controversies: A study of value conflicts in education.* Unpublished doctoral dissertation, Virginia Polytechnic Institute and State University, Blacksburg.

Edwards, J. (1983). What's moral about "The catcher in the rye?" *English Journal 72*(4), 39–42.

Edwards, J. (1985). "I know why the caged bird sings": Awareness of displacement. In N. J. Karolides & L. Burress (Eds.), *Celebrating the censored book!* (pp. 61–63). Racine, WI: Wisconsin Council of Teachers of English.

Engel v. Vitale, 8 L.Ed.2d 601 (1962).

Erikson, E. (1968). *Identity, youth and crisis.* New York: Norton.

Etzioni, A. (1996). In character education, virtue should be seen, not just heard. *Education Week 15*(36), 40, 31.

Everson v. Board of Education, 330 U.S. 1 (1946).

The faces of the Christian Coalition. [Poster]. Washington, DC: People for the American Way. (n.d.)

Facing history or censoring it? (1989, Winter). *Forum.* People for the American Way newsletter, p. 7.

Falwell, J. (1980). *Listen, America!.* Garden City, NY: Doubleday.

Falwell, J. (1982). *Finding inner strength and peace.* Garden City, NY: Doubleday.

Falwell, J. (1983, September). Who is responsible for educating children? *Fundamentalist Journal,* p. 8.

Falwell, J. (1992). *The new American family.* Dallas, TX: Word.

Finch, P. (1983). *God, guts, and guns.* New York: Seaview/Putnam.

Foerstel, H. N. (1994). *Banned in the U.S.A.: A reference guide to book censorship in schools and public libraries.* Westport, CT: Greenwood.

Frohnmayer, J. (1994). *Out of tune: Listening to the First Amendment.* Nashville, TN: The Freedom Forum First Amendment Center, Vanderbilt University.

Frye, N. (1971). *The educated imagination* (6th ed.). Bloomington: Indiana University Press.

Frymier, J., Cunningham, L., Duckett, W., Gansneder, B., Link, F., Rimmer, J., & Scholz, J. (1995). *Values on which we agree.* Bloomington, IN: Phi Delta Kappa.

Gabler, M. & Gabler, N. (1985). *What are they teaching our children?* Wheaton, IL: Victor.

Gardner, J. (1983). *On becoming a novelist.* New York: Harper & Row.

Hardy, T. (1965). *Tess of the D'Urbervilles* (Reprint of 5th edition). New York: Airmont. (Original work published 1892)

Hefley, J. C. (1977). *Textbooks on trial.* Wheaton, IL: Victor.

Hentoff, N. (1987, September 3). Why teach us to read and then say we can't? *The Washington Post,* p. 15.

Herberg, W. (1974). America's civil religion: What it is and whence it comes. In R. E. Richey & D. G. Jones (Eds.), *American civil religion* (pp. 76–88). New York: Harper & Row.

Hoffman, R. J., & Larue, G. A. (Eds.). (1988). *Biblical v. secular ethics.* Buffalo, NY: Prometheus.

The Holy Bible (1995). King James Version. Grand Rapids, WI: Zondervan.

Homstad, W. (1995). *Anatomy of a book controversy.* Bloomington, IN: Phi Delta Kappa Educational Foundation.

Irving, D. (1963). *The destruction of Dresden.* New York: Holt, Rinehart & Winston.

Jackson, J. H. (1953). Introduction. In *The short novels of John Steinbeck* (p. viii). New York: Viking.

Johnson, H. (1997). Warning: Severe sessions ahead. *Church and State 50*(1), 8.

Kaplan, G. R. (1994). Shotgun wedding: Notes on public education's encounter with the new Christian right. *Phi Delta Kappan Special Report, 75*(9), K7.

Kaufman, L. (1994, October 16). Life beyond God. *The New York Times Magazine,* 49.

Kilpatrick, W., Wolfe, G., & Wolfe, S. M. (1994). *Books that build character: A guide to teaching your child moral values through stories.* New York: Simon & Schuster.

Kosinski, J. (1976). Against book censorship. *Media and Methods 12*(5), 22–24.

Kramnick, I., & Moore, R. L. (1996). *The godless Constitution: The case against religious correctness.* New York: Norton.

Kropp, A. J. (1987, July 20). Religious right cashing in on AIDS epidemic. *The Houston Post,* p. 4.

Kushner, H. S. (1981). *When bad things happen to good people.* New York: Schocken.

Kushner, H. S. (1986). *When all you've ever wanted isn't enough.* New York: Summit.

Kushner, H. S. (1989). *Who needs God.* New York: Summit.

LaHaye, T. (1980). *What everyone should know about homosexuality.* Wheaton, IL: Tyndale House.

LaHaye, T. (1982). *The battle for the family.* Old Tappan, NJ: Fleming H. Revell.

LaHaye, T. (1983). *The battle for the public schools.* Old Tappan, NJ: Fleming H. Revell.

LaHaye, T. (1992). *No fear of the storm.* Sisters, OR: Multnomah.

LaHaye, T., & LaHaye, B. (1978). *Spirit-controlled family living.* Old Tappan, NJ: Fleming H. Revell.

LaHaye, T. & LaHaye, B. (1993). *Against the tide: How to raise sexually pure kids in an "anything goes" world.* Sisters, OR: Multnomah.

Lamont, C. (1982). *The philosophy of humanism* (6th ed.). New York: Frederick Ungar. (Original work published 1949)

Larson, M. A. (1984). *Jefferson: Magnificent populist.* Greenwich, CT: Devin-Adair.

Lee, H. (1982). *To kill a mockingbird.* New York: Warner.

Lemon v. Kurtzman, 29 L.Ed.2d 745 (1971).

Levy, L. W. (1981). *Treason against God: A history of the offense of blasphemy.* New York: Schocken.

Levy, L. W. (1986). *The establishment clause: Religion and the First Amendment.* New York: Macmillan.

Mack, B. (1995). *Who wrote the New Testament?: The making of the Christian myth.* New York: HarperCollins.

Maguire, D. C. (1982). *The new subversives.* New York: Continuum.

Maguire, D. C. (1986). *The moral revolution: A Christian humanist vision.* New York: Harper & Row.

Maguire, D. C. (1993). *The moral core of Judaism and Christianity: Reclaiming the revolution.* Minneapolis, MN: Fortress.

Martin, W. (1982, November). The guardians who slumbereth not. *The Texas Monthly,* 145–151, 267–271.

Marty, M. E. (1987). *Religion and republic: The American circumstance.* Boston: Beacon.

McDonald, J. (1988) *A dictionary of obscenity, taboo and euphemism.* London: Sphere.

Meeks, W. A. (1986). *The moral world of the first Christians.* Philadelphia: Westminster.

Mizner D. A. (1996). A fright show. *Church and State 49*(1), 10–13.

Montague, A. (1967). *The anatomy of swearing.* New York: Macmillan.

Most Americans say right and wrong is all relative. (1992, April 4). *The Milwaukee Journal,* p. A4.

Moyers, B. (1995). Echoes of the crusades. *Church and State 48*(11), 16–19.

Mozert v. Hawkins County, TN, Board of Education. 827 F.2d 1058 (U.S.Ct.App., 6th Cir., 1987).

Niebuhr, R. (1960). *The children of light and the children of darkness.* New York: Charles Scribner's Sons.

Nord, W. (1996). *Religion and American education: Rethinking a national dilemma.* Chapel Hill: University of North Carolina Press.

Packard, W. (Ed.). (1974). *The craft of poetry.* Garden City, NY: Doubleday.

Padover, S. K. (Ed.). (1953). *Thomas Jefferson on democracy.* New York: D. Appleton-Century. (Original work published 1939)

Parini, J. (1992, September 27). Of bindlestiffs, bad times, mice and men. *The New York Times,* p. 24H.

Parker, F. (1975). *The battle of the books: Kanawha County.* Bloomington, IN: Phi Delta Kappa fastback.

Paterson, K. (1981). *Gates of excellence: On reading and writing books for children.* New York: Elsevier/Nelson.

Peck, M. S. (1978). *The road less traveled: A new psychology of love, traditional values and spiritual growth.* New York: Simon & Schuster.

Perry, R. B. (1944). *Puritanism and democracy.* New York: Vanguard.

Pfeffer, L. (1958). *Creeds in competition: A creative force in American culture.* New York: Harper & Row.

Ralph Reed endorsement of prophecy book could hurt Catholic Alliance recruitment. (1996). *Church and State 49*(11), 14.

Rawson, H. (1989). *Wicked words: A treasury of curses, insults, put-downs, and other formerly unprintable terms from Anglo-Saxon times to the present.* New York: Crown.

The Rebirth of America. (1986). Valley Forge, PA: The Arthur S. DeMoss Foundation.

Reed, R. (1994). *Politically incorrect: The emerging faith factor in American politics.* Dallas, TX: Word.

Reed, R. (1996). *Active faith: How Christians are changing the soul of American politics.* New York: The Free Press.

Reich, D. (1994). Keeping tabs on the right. *The World 9*(2), 14.

Religious right gears up for elections. (1988, Fall). *Forum.* People for the American Way newsletter, p. 1.

Reunzel, D. (1996). Old time religion. *Education Week 15* (27), 31–35.

Riley, R. (1995). Statement of principles—schools and religion (p. 1). Washington, DC: Department of Education.

Robertson, P. (1984). *Answers to 200 of life's most probing questions.* Nashville, TN: Thomas Nelson.

Robertson, P. (1991). *The new world order.* Dallas, TX: Word.

Robertson, P. (1993). *The turning tide: The fall of liberalism and the rise of common sense.* Dallas, TX: Word.

Robinson. W. V. (1987, December 5). Co-chairmen for Kemp rap Jews, Catholics. *The Boston Globe*, p. 1.

Safire, W. (1986, January 29). An etymologist peers at secular humanism. *The Milwaukee Journal*, Part 1, p. 13.

Salinger, J. D. (1957). *The catcher in the rye.* New York: Signet.

Salk, L. (1990, April 15). The American family is alive and well...but under attack. *Bottom Line*, p. 9.

Schlafly, P. (1984). *Child abuse in the classroom.* Alton, IL: Pere Marquette.

Seldes, G. [Compiler] (1985). *The great thoughts.* New York: Ballantine.

Simmons, J. E. (Ed.) (1994). *Censorship: A threat to reading, learning, thinking.* Newark, DE: International Reading Association.

Smart, J. D. (1977). *The cultural subversion of the biblical faith.* Philadelphia: Westminster Press.

Some want U.S. called Christian nation. (1996, August 17). *The Daily Star*, Oneonta, NY, p. 9.

Spong, J. S. (1991). *Rescuing the Bible from the fundamentalists: A bishop rethinks the meaning of scripture.* New York: HarperCollins.

Steinbeck J. (1953). *Of mice and men.* In *The short novels of John Steinbeck.* New York: Viking. (Original work published 1937)

Steinbeck, J. (1969). *The grapes of wrath.* New York: Bantam. (Original work published 1939)

Storr, A. (1988) *Solitude: A return to the self.* New York: The Free Press.

Torcaso v. Watkins, 6 L.Ed.2d, 982. (1961).

U.S. v. Schwimmer, U.S. Sup. Ct. Reports, 644 (1928).

Veix, D. B. (1975). Teaching a censored novel: Slaughterhouse five. *English Journal 64*(7), 25–33.

Vonnegut, K. (1966). *Slaughterhouse-five.* New York: Dell.

Wallace v. Jaffree, 86 L.Ed.2d, 29 (1985).

West, C. (1994). *Race matters.* New York: Vintage.

West, M. I. (1988) *Trust your children: Voices against censorship in children's literature.* New York: Neal-Schuman.

Author Index

Subject Index